1992

W9-AFO-202

3 0301 00054054 8

Anglo-Saxon Manuscripts

MICHELLE P. BROWN

University of Toronto Press

College of St. Francis Library
Joliet, Illinois

Front cover: detail from The Vespasian Psalter, f.30v; *see* **59**.

Back cover: see **49**.

Title-page: **The Royal Bible**
9th cent., second quarter; Canterbury (St Augustine's ?).

Opening of St Luke's Gospel, from a fragmentary Gospels, probably originally a Bible. Its purple pages, gold and silver script and illusionistic painting style are ultimately reminiscent of Mediterranean (especially Byzantine) works, although a product of the Carolingian Court School probably furnished the immediate inspiration and English 'Tiberius' group decoration is added.
British Library, Royal MS 1.E.VI, f.43.

This page: detail from **69**.

Opposite: detail from **16**.

First published 1991 by
The British Library
First published in North America 1991 by
University of Toronto Press
Toronto and Buffalo

ISBN 0-8020-7728-5

Designed by Roger Davies
Set on Ventura by The Green Street Press
Colour origination by York House Graphics
Printed in England by Jolly & Barber, Rugby

091
B879

Contents

144,444

Introduction

The Anglo-Saxons entered the historical scene in the 5th century as pagan Germanic pirates and mercenaries, accompanied by their camp-followers. This was part of a much wider movement of 'barbarian' peoples (those living beyond the frontiers of Roman territory) who forced their way into the Empire, stimulated by a variety of motives. By the time of the Norman Conquest in 1066 Anglo-Saxon England was one of the most sophisticated states of the medieval West, renowned for its cultural and ecclesiastical achievements and possessing complex administrative, legal and financial structures, many aspects of which were preserved by the new Norman élite.

Command of the written word, in addition to a well-developed oral tradition, was of tremendous importance in this transformation. The Anglo-Saxons were introduced to a full system of literacy as part of the process of conversion to Christianity, an enterprise launched by both the Celtic and Roman Churches, with some Gaulish participation, in the late 6th century. Within a century they and their Celtic neighbours had transformed the book into a rich vehicle for their distinctive art and culture, which was to exert an influence throughout the Middle Ages and beyond (1).

The Anglo-Saxon period may perhaps usefully be viewed as a series of phases: firstly, the sub-Roman and Migration period (early 5th to late 6th century); secondly, the Insular period (later 6th to mid-9th century); thirdly, the Alfredian renewal (late 9th century); fourthly, the later Anglo-Saxon period (10th and 11th centuries, to 1066).

Each phase brought new developments to the history of the book. The sub-Roman period witnessed a certain level of continuity of the literacy of Antiquity, through the agency of the Church. In the face of the pagan Germanic onslaught the indigenous British Church largely retreated into the 'Highland zone' (modern 'Celtdom'). It participated actively in the conversion of Ireland where a distinctive Christian culture emerged, noted for its learning and

1 The Book of Durrow

Late 7th cent.; Iona, or Ireland or Northumbria (?).

Carpet page from the first of the great illuminated Insular Gospel-books. It combines Germanic, Celtic, Pictish, Mediterranean and eastern influences (with Germanic interlace being here combined with Celtic spiralwork in a form of Coptic decorated page). Its date and origin are hotly disputed. Textually it relates closely to the controversial Book of Kells (*see* **61, 62**).

Dublin, Trinity College Library, MS 57, f.3v.

influenced by its Celtic and British legacies and those of the eastern Mediterranean, Gaul and Spain. Episcopal and monastic organizations were adopted, Latin was learnt systematically as a new language, and a system of scripts was developed, free from the vulgarization often experienced in areas of the old Empire (of which Ireland had never formed a part). The earliest surviving books from these islands (such as Codex Usserianus Primus and the Springmount Bog Tablets) were produced in Ireland, probably during the early 7th century (**2**).

In England the resistance to the Germanic advance, associated with Ambrosius Aurelianus and the historically elusive figure of Arthur (**4**), had collapsed by the second half of the 6th century (as lamented by Gildas (**3**)) and by *c*.600 a myriad of small Anglo-Saxon political units had been established, out of which several larger kingdoms emerged. Of these Kent, Essex, Sussex, Wessex, East Anglia, Northumbria (Deira and Bernicia) and Mercia assumed prominence. Pockets of indigenous British settlement and some kingdoms (notably Strathclyde, Rheged and Elmet) survived, but the bulk of the population were forced into Wales, Cornwall and southern Scotland, whilst many migrated to Brittany.

The task of converting the Anglo-Saxons was undertaken on two fronts: by the Celtic Church, established in the Irish kingdom of Dal Riada in Argyll (notably at Iona) and extending its missionary activity throughout Scotland and

2 The Springmount Bog Tablets
Early 7th cent.; Ireland.

Reusable wax tablets were widely used from Antiquity almost until the present. They were often used for drafting, teaching, accounting and both informal and formal purposes. These tablets carry excerpts from the Psalms and were perhaps being studied by a trainee priest before being lost in a bog in Co. Antrim. They carry one of the earliest survivals of Insular handwriting.

Dublin, National Museum of Ireland, S.A.1914:2.

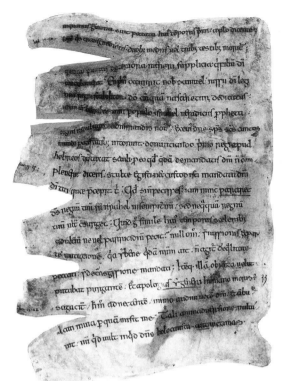

4 Nennius, *Historia Brittonum*
*c.*1100; ?

This is the earliest copy of a history of the British written by a Welsh ecclesiastic, *c.*830, who is often known as Nennius. A *pot pourri* of material, it is highly 'romantic' in character and contains much of the early elaboration on the theme of Arthur. Here an account of his alleged battles, including the important British victory at Mount Badon, is given.

British Library, Harley MS 3859, f.187.

3 Gildas, *De Excidio Brianniae et Conquestu*
10th cent.; Canterbury, St Augustine's (?)

The earliest surviving copy of *The Ruin and Conquest of Britain*, composed in the mid-6th century by a British monk named Gildas. It is a polemical partial narration of the early history of Britain, with specific reference to the Germanic invasions (which are attributed to moral laxity on the part of the British and their rulers).

British Library, Cotton MS Vitellius A.VI, f.16v.

into England, and by the Roman Church through the mission of St Augustine to Kent in 597 (**5**). Despite certain differences in religious observation, which were discussed at the famous Synod of Whitby in 664 and settled in favour of the Roman mainstream, members of both groups worked together on the process of conversion within England, the Germanic homelands and elsewhere on the Continent. So akin were the cultures of Britain and Ireland at this stage that the term 'Insular' is often applied, indicating a level of shared cultural identity throughout the islands, although each area retained its own distinctive character.

During the 7th century the Christian culture of Anglo-Saxon England took shape, given substance by the formalization of an ecclesiastical structure throughout England by Archbishop Theodore, a Greek-speaking monk from Tarsus in Asia Minor, who was appointed to Canterbury in his 60s and was in office from 669 to 690.

Theodore and his colleague from Africa, Hadrian, Abbot of St Augustine's, established a remarkable school at Canterbury which revolutionized learning in England, bringing Mediterranean influence to bear upon a curriculum which focused upon metre (poetic composition), computus (the study of chronology) and astronomy, as well as the study of Scripture (**6**).

Such a curriculum was also adopted in the romanizing foundations of Northumbria, notably the twin monasteries of Monkwearmouth (674) and Jarrow (682). The brightest star in this scholarly firmament was Bede (673–735), who entered Jarrow as a child and remained there, with very rare sorties, for the remainder of a remarkable working life (**9**).

The works of Anglo-Saxon scholars such as Aldhelm and Bede were immediate 'bestsellers'. Correspondence of the period contains numerous requests for copies of these, and liturgical books, especially via the Continent. Both Irish and English religious personnel had carried their faith to the Continent from the 7th century, founding monasteries such as Luxeuil,

5 The Augustine Gospels
*c.*600; Rome.

Portrait of St Luke, his symbol and flanking scenes from the life of Christ. It belongs to a linear style of Late Antique illumination which was to influence the Insular approach in works such as the Lindisfarne Gospels. It travelled to St Augustine's, Canterbury, (where it apparently inspired manuscripts such as the Stockholm Codex Aureus (*see* **68**)) and is traditionally associated with St Augustine's mission of 597.
Cambridge, Corpus Christi College, MS 286, f.129v.

6 Glossary
Mid-10th cent.; Canterbury, St Augustine's.

Glossaries provide explanations, and perhaps a translation, of certain terms. These might be drawn from specific texts or be subject-based, as is this example which includes the Latin names for types of fish, with their Old English equivalents (e.g. *sardina = hæring*). These teaching aids were promoted in England, especially by Theodore and the Canterbury school, from the 7th century onwards.
British Library, Cotton MS Cleopatra A.III, f.77.

hneahe mus	zloe
Verpentilia	**P** lætipa
znæt	peoloc
S emper	**C** oclea
myze	hacod
C ulix	**L** uciur
perp	flip
V erpis	**T** metur
peld beo	hpæl
A dticur	**C** octur
beo	pipe
A pir	**P** ipcip
fifealde	hylon hpon
P ampilio	**B** allena.t pilina
hypneta	mepofpm
C pabpio	**D** elpin
mirchpepn	mepe fpm
N octacopax	**B** acharpus
pypel	peolh
S canebiur	**F** ocur
hpeohbita	fypuzæ
B latta	**P** opcopifcip
ceapor	leax
B puchur	**I** pic
zænphoppe	ofpe
L ocufta	**O** rtpea
emel	myxle
C upculio	**G** enipcula
hama	hæpepn
C icada	**C** ancep
	hæping
I ncipit	**S** apoina
	beny
DE PISCIBUS:	**L** upur

mat
the
us.
euang

mar
cus.
euang

lu
cas.
euang

Ioh
an
nis.
euang

thomas scribsit

7 The Trier Gospels
8th cent., second quarter; Echternach.

The Tetramorph - a conflation of the evangelist symbols, an unparalleled image probably intended to emphasise the unity of the Gospels. The Trier Gospels were written by two scribes one of whom, the Thomas whose name appears here, was English. During the 8th century, Echternach, an Insular foundation in Luxembourg, drew stylistically upon various sources: Insular, Continental and Antique.

Trier, Domschatz, Cod.61, f.5v.

8 (opposite) The Synod of Clofesho, 803
9th cent., first half; Canterbury.

Account of an important ecclesiastical meeting at which Offa's third archbishopric of Lichfield (designed to ensure greater royal control of the Church) was dismantled and its privileges restored to Canterbury. This synod marked the beginning of the southern see's reaction against lay control. The form of the document resembles that of charters, which at this period would be produced by, or on behalf of, the recipients, with a copy being retained by both parties. The script is a 'mannered minuscule' of Canterbury type.

British Library, Cotton MS Augustus II.61.

St Gall and Bobbio (Columbanus), Echternach (Willibrord) **(7)** and Fulda (Boniface) **(19)**. These centres continued to receive recruits from their homelands and made a positive contribution to Continental learning, culminating in the Carolingian 'renaissance' of the late 8th to 9th centuries, in which Charlemagne was assisted by one of the most learned churchmen of his day, Alcuin of York (*c.*735–804). Alcuin tells us that the York library was among the finest of the age, but alas, no surviving books of the period may be convincingly attributed to it, indicating how much has been lost.

The ascendancy enjoyed by Northumbria during much of the 7th century gave way to that of Mercia under Kings Aethelbald (716–57), Offa (757–96) and Coenwulf (796–821), who extended their authority throughout much of an often unwilling Southumbria. The manuscripts and other works of art produced south of the Humber during this time exhibit a taste for Mediterranean and Oriental influences and there is evidence of complex relations with the Carolingian Empire **(10)**. The latter trend was cultivated by the southern English ecclesiastics, notably the formidable Archbishop of Canterbury, Wulfred (805–32), partly as an aid to combatting secular control of the monasteries **(8)**.

A Mercia weakened by dissent had yielded its supremacy to Wessex, under King Egbert (802–39), by 830. The middle years of the 9th century witnessed continuing Carolingian relations, but increasingly attention was focused upon a new threat – the Vikings.

Lindisfarne fell prey to the first Scandinavian attack in 793, sending shock-waves throughout the West. In 865 the first great Viking army arrived and by 870 only Wessex effectively continued to resist.

The reign of Alfred the Great (871-99) witnessed progressive Viking invasion and settlement, which he eventually managed to check, symbolized by his treaty (drawn up between 886 and 890) with Guthrum, leader of the Danes in East Anglia. This partitioned England

...loqui hæreticis... et... pro hominibus bonæ uoluntatis.

† Scimus autem quod multis in christi ecclesiæ contemplatoribus notum et manifestum est... et nihil tam sibi illud placabile...

[The main body of this document is a medieval Latin charter/council record written in an Anglo-Saxon minuscule hand, largely concerning Æðelheard archiepiscopus and the synod, dated to the incarnation of the Lord and indiction, held at the place called Clofesho.]

...Anno illo dominicæ incarnationis .dccc.iii. indictione .xi. die .iiii. iduum octobris. Ego Æðelheard archiepiscopus cum omnibus...

...Hæc sunt nomina episcoporum et abbatum qui præscriptam cyrographam cartulam in synodo qui factus est æt Clofeshoum anno dominicæ incarnationis .dccc.iii. cum signo sanctæ crucis christi firmauerunt.

† Æðelheard archiepiscopus.

† Aldulfus epis.	† Alhmundus epis.	† Uuihthunus epis.	† Beorna pbr. ab.
† ...bisceux epis.	† Eymundus epis.	† Uulpheius epis.	† ...pbr. ab.
† Alhheardus epis.	† Alduulfus epis.	† ...epis.	† ...undus pbr. ab.
† ...bisceax epis.	† ...bischtus epis.	† Alhmundus pbr. ab.	

Ita cis septentrionlin & occidentlin
loc. tcc est. Ghmacmicæ gellicæ
hispanicæ. maximis euro pote
pceribus·

Multo st dismello æculin sæ. quoce
plzmiljæ pæssum·Dccc·Inbone
cem longe lætitudinis habet miljæ
ccc Geecptir dum texeat pliolixio
ubus diuexorum pno moitto uio
ium tiocetibur·

Quibus septietur ut emeutas bus
queednexig octes·lxxv·miljæ com
pleatt·habet cambuchæ gelljcem
belgcæm cuius pnoximum ltais
tiochis mecaris br· æpsius ciuitacs que
dictam rtubi portus·

Æstice cardonum puue coniupræ
insptæ ccestin uo cærtæ·

Ista post tomaciu ætpsponiæeo
morunonium chitis litone pnovimo
tiocisetumilium quin quæ gittæ
siue ut quidam scripshis & tæeci
orum ccccl₃

Atchico hrunde oceano Inpinto
patis oncædeas Insulas habet·
Optimæ purisbus atque ombonibus
lusulæ & calsudis æptæ pcconibs·

A quadraginta· octo meibus piumno· est que miljæ stinghtræ mihæ piæ
Ist is cailly hpus surendi· piseluud mila

9 Bede, *Historia Ecclesiastica*

9th cent. (820s-30s ?); Kent (Canterbury)
(or Mercia) ?

Opening of Book I of Bede's *History
of the English Church and People* or
Ecclesiastical History, composed at
Jarrow and completed in 731. An
early medieval 'best-seller', of which
this is an early (but not the earliest)
copy. In this work Bede introduced a
new concept of historiography, in
which cause and effect were
perceived and a consistent system of
dating (from the Incarnation of
Christ) was promoted. The
'Tiberius' group of southern English
manuscripts takes its name from this
book. Its ornament resembles
'Trewhiddle style' metalwork.

*British Library, Cotton MS Tiberius C.II,
f.5v.*

10 The Barberini Gospels

Late 8th cent.; Mercia, or perhaps York
or Northumbria (?).

Opening of St Mark's Gospel. Four
scribes worked on this book, the
master scribe of which may have
been the Wigbald mentioned in the
colophon. At least one member of
the team was probably a Mercian,
working alongside more experienced
scribes of Northumbrian training.
The illumination exhibits
Italo-Byzantine influence consistent
with that found in other Mercian
works of the period (e.g. the
sculptures at Breedon-on-the-Hill,
Leics.).

*Vatican City, Biblioteca Apostolica
Vaticana, MS Barb. lat. 570, f.51.*

11 Alfred's Preface to the _Pastoral Care_
_c_.890-7; Winchester (?).

Composed by Pope Gregory the Great (590-604), the _Pastoral Care_ deals with the spiritual and intellectual abilities required to govern with. It was translated into English by Alfred himself, and his preface contains a lament on the decline of learning and an appeal to his bishops to assist in renewal (this copy addressed to Werferth, Bishop of Worcester). As an added incentive a precious _aestel_, thought perhaps to have been a book pointer, was sent and is referred to here.

Oxford, Bodleian Library, Hatton MS 20, f.2v.

revival of book-learning (and thereby spiritual renewal) included a policy of translation into Old English of works of particular relevance to the situation (_see_ **11, 27**).

A turning point had been reached in English literacy: a degree of preservation of older Insular culture was established, Continental influence became even more of a feature of Anglo-Saxon culture, and new trends in vernacular literacy were developed. Likewise, on the political front the scene was set for the next phase of English history, dominated by the reconquest of the Danelaw and a new sense of national unity. By the end of his reign Athelstan (925–39) had begun to assert the rule of a single monarchy throughout England and into southern Scotland and Wales, this new-found stability permitting him to engage in a series of diplomatic relations with the Continent and to indulge his love of art and learning, with the acquisition of works, relics and influences from varied sources (_see_ **12, 25, 69**).

The second half of the 10th century saw the introduction of a major campaign for monastic reform, along Continental lines, favouring (theoretically) the wholesale observance of the Rule of St Benedict (**70**) (prior to this those in charge of individual religious establishments could generally determine their own observance). Under the patronage of King Edgar (959–75) (**14**) three great reforming prelates operated: Dunstan, Archbishop of Canterbury (960–88), Aethelwold, Bishop of Winchester (963–84) and Oswald, Bishop of Worcester (961–92; also Archbishop of York, 971–92). Reform was formalized in the _Regularis Concordia_ (between 963 and 975), a written agreement of monastic uniformity within the English Church (in theory, if not in practice), and 973 saw Edgar's coronation in Bath, celebrated with a new ritual perhaps imbued with imperial connotations (**13**). This period of collaboration between Church and State witnessed a spectacular flowering of the arts, Dunstan and Aethelwold themselves being accomplished craftsmen, with no shortage of patronage.

into the Danelaw (Northumbria, East Anglia and the 'Five Boroughs', incorporating much of Mercia) and 'English' England, the latter preserving Wessex, and the territory south of the Thames, and the south-western part of Mercia. The other issue which most preoccupied Alfred was the religious and cultural degeneracy of England, to which its woes were attributed (**11**). He recruited a scholarly team composed of Mercians (Werferth, Plegmund, Werwulf and Aethelstan), a Welshman (Asser) and two Continental scholars (Grimbald of St Bertin and John the Old Saxon). The programme for the

12 Bede's Lives of St Cuthbert

c.934; south-western England.

King Athelstan says 'this is your life' to St Cuthbert.
Athelstan was a notable patron of the arts and
presented many gifts to the shrine of St Cuthbert,
then at Chester-le-Street, which he visited in 934.
This book was probably made as a result of this visit
and reflects Athelstan's attempts to secure West
Saxon rule in northern England.

Cambridge, Corpus Christi College, MS 183, f.1v.

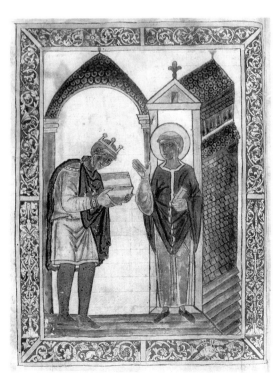

13 The *Regularis Concordia*

c.1050; Canterbury, Christ Church.

This miniature symbolizes the monastic reform
movement. King Edgar is shown, flanked by the
reformers Dunstan and Aethelwold, whilst the monk
below represents the submission of the English
Church to Benedictinism, embodied in the *Regularis
Concordia*, or assent to the Benedictine Rule, of *c*.970.

British Library, Cotton MS Tiberius A.III, f.2v.

14   The New Minster Charter

c.966; Winchester, New Minster.

This frontispiece to King Edgar's charter to the New Minster, commemorating its adoption of Benedictinism, is the earliest example of the fully painted 'Winchester' style. Edgar is shown, between the Virgin and St Peter, presenting the charter to Christ.

British Library, Cotton MS Vespasian A.VIII, f.2v.

The late 10th and early 11th centuries witnessed renewed disruption, with succession crises, conflict between pro- and anti-reform parties, alliance with Normandy and weak government under Ethelred II 'Unræd', the 'ill-advised' (978–1016). Scandinavian intervention recommenced, this time associated with the ambitions of a centralized Danish monarchy, resulting in the accession of Cnut (1016–35). England became part of a northern, Scandinavian Empire: peace was assured (formalized by Cnut's social contract with the English, of 1019-20, in which protection was pledged in return for allegiance) and the arts once again flourished, patronized by the king and his wives (**15**).

Succession conflicts followed Cnut's death (**16**), culminating in the accession of Edward 'the Confessor' (1042–66), another patron of the arts. However, instability had permitted the English earls to grow overmighty. Upon Edward's death his brother-in-law, Harold Godwine, Earl of Wessex, seized the throne (despite the claims of Edward's ally, William of Normandy). His reign lasted less than a year, during which the threads of international relations woven during the preceding years took substance in the events narrated by the Bayeux Tapestry. With the Norman Conquest of 1066 the political reality of Anglo-Saxon England came to an end. Fortunately its cultural identity did not.

The testimony of Domesday Book, a phenomenal property survey drawn up towards the end of William I's reign (1066–87) charts the fall of the Anglo-Saxons. Only two major English landholders are recorded and by 1087 there was only one English bishop and two significant abbots. Nevertheless, this should not lead to an under-estimation of the continuing Anglo-Saxon contribution. The arts, including those of the book, continued to reflect and build upon English influence, even if new texts were introduced, sometimes supplanting their precursors (especially in the field of ecclesiastical service-books), and many aspects (some of which are with us still) of the imposing administrative structure with which the Normans and their Angevin successors ruled their extensive empires were firmly rooted in the Anglo-Saxon world (**17**). Anglo-Saxon influence was far from ended and certainly played an important role in moulding the literacy, art, culture and administration of the medieval, and thereby the modern world.

16   The *Encomium* of Queen Emma
Mid-11th cent.; Normandy.

A biography *cum* 'apology' of Emma, wife successively of Ethelred II and Cnut. Her role in events following Cnut's death, during which one of her sons by Ethelred, Alfred, died, seems to have necessitated some vindication. She is shown receiving the work, watched by her sons, Harthacnut and Edward (the Confessor). An indebtedness to English manuscripts may be seen in this Norman work.
British Library, Add. MS 33241, ff.1v-2.

17   Writ of Edward the Confessor
1052.

The royal and private letter (*gewrit*), authenticated by a seal, was known in England from the later 9th century (although only examples from the 11th century onwards survive). Writs were important administrative instruments, conveying royal instructions to local representatives, and could also, in conjunction with charters, record grants. This specimen gives notification of a grant of territorial and financial jurisdiction to Christ Church, Canterbury. The body of the text, other than the first three lines, was rewritten in the 12th century, a common practice. The Normans continued to use writs and by the 13th century they had developed into 'letters patent and close', through which medieval England was administered. The 'majesty portrait' on the seal, depicting the King, was derived from Ottonian models.
British Library, Campbell Charter XXI.5.

15   The New Minster *Liber Vitae*
1031 (?); Winchester, New Minster.

This frontispiece, to a book listing those commemorated by the New Minster and Hyde Abbey, depicts Cnut and his wife, Aelfgyfu, presenting a cross to Christ and the community. The book was written by the scribe Aelsinus.
British Library, Stowe MS 944, f.6.

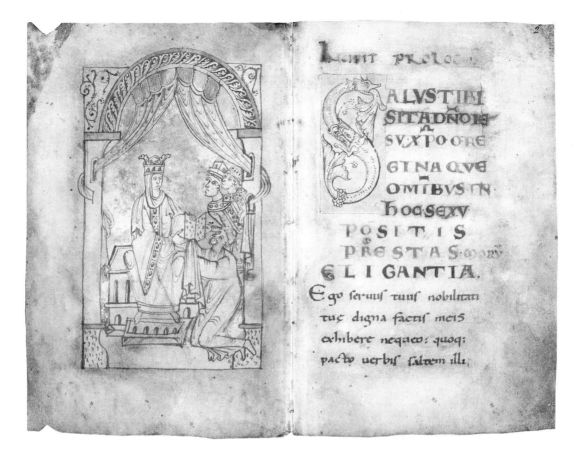

INCIPIT PROLOGVS

SALVSTIBI
SIT A DNO IS
SVX PO ORE
GINA QVE
OMIBVS IN
hoc SEXV
POSITIS
PRESTAS cornu
ELIGANTIA.

Ego seruus tuus nobilitati
tuç digna factis meis
exhibere nequeo: quoq;
pacto uerbis saltem illi

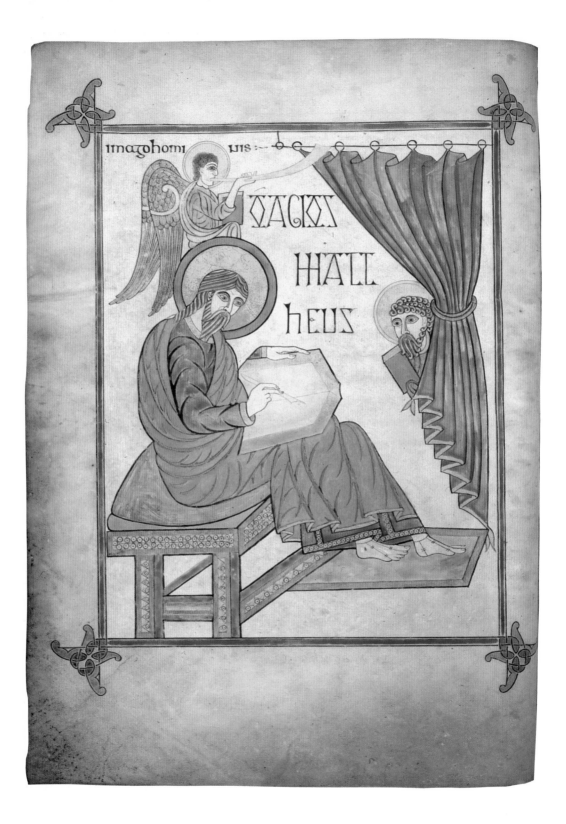

Book production and consumption

18   The Lindisfarne Gospels

*c.*700; Lindisfarne.

St Matthew accompanied by his symbol and a peeping figure, perhaps derived from an Antique image of the Poet and his Muse. The miniature was probably adapted from that of Ezra in the Codex Amiatinus (*see* **49**), or, more likely, from its Mediterranean model. The text of this copy of the Gospels displays Neapolitan features.

British Library, Cotton MS Nero D.IV, f.25v.

It is generally assumed that, from the demise of the Roman Empire until the rise of the western universities (around AD 1200), which generated a growth in secular commercialized book production to accommodate the demands of a broader literate public, book production was the province of the monasteries. This was broadly the case, although there are signs of continued secular production of documents elsewhere in medieval Europe and there remains the possibility of limited lay participation in book production. Within the sphere of ecclesiastical production it should not be assumed that permanent attachment to a single scriptorium (or 'writing office') was entailed - the manuscripts themselves yield plenty of evidence that scribes and artists, as well as their works and exemplars, were mobile. Furthermore, writing was not confined to those whose talents meant that their *opus dei*, or 'work for God' (an integral part of the monastic day as prescribed, for example, within the monastic rule composed by Cassiodorus), consisted largely of book production. Many churchmen who were not 'professional' monastic scribes (such as Boniface, Willibrord, Aelfric and Wulfstan) have nonetheless left specimens of their hands in marginal annotations (**19, 20, 21**). It should be recognized that, in a period when book production was a manual activity, 'literacy' might not necessarily entail the ability to write; works might be dictated to a competent scribe, even by notable scholars of the later Middle Ages. This is perhaps akin to modern computer literacy: those who can digest the written word, or even compose texts, might not personally possess the ability to use the technology for generating formal writing themselves, or might do so merely in a limited fashion.

Assessing the extent of literacy (even in a restricted, conventional sense meaning the ability to read and write) in Anglo-Saxon England is extremely difficult, given the nature of the sources. Class may well have been the primary determining factor, with the upper echelons of society enjoying a higher, if restricted access to

aliquan do medio tempore. aliquando desola
ipsa persecutione. aut non multo ante dicitur
ne capitulat; nunc ergo discribta orexta ad o
riginem redit. eadem breuiter aliter que
dicitur ut VII portae in qua uidi quattu
or angelor stantes per quattuor angulor
terrae. tenentes quattuor uentos terrae
ne in terra flarent. neuelnmari. neuelnulla ar
bore; inqua quattuor angelis ira regna quatta
ordesignatu aecclesiainIohan ne cognosceret
et istiorum. et medo rum ex pensorum et romar
norum, qui suo quodam modo potentia ar om
nia praepotentar; nullum prohibeto ranitur
sinerent nespirare; Ideo neIn terra Inquid
flarent. idest habitantar; neuelnmari neue

19 Primasius, *on the Apocalypse,* with notes by St Boniface

Late 7th cent.; England, or an English centre on the Continent.

The text is written in a Phase I half-uncial script, with annotations in a Southumbrian Phase I minuscule, probably written by the famous English missionary and martyr, St Boniface (died 754), the 'Apostle of Germany'.

Oxford, Bodleian Library, Douce MS 140, f.59v.

20 Aelfric, *First Series of Catholic Homilies*

*c.*990; Cerne Abbey, Dorset.

Aelfric (died *c.*1020), Abbot of Cerne, was, along with Wulfstan, an important author of Old English prose and a champion of the reform movement during the late 10th–11th centuries. His homilies form a two-year cycle of his own preaching material, published for use by other priests. Annotations by Aelfric himself.

British Library, Royal MS 7.C.XII, f.105.

21 Wulfstan, *Sermon of the Wolf to the English*

Early 11th cent.; Worcester or York (?).

Wulfstan, Bishop of London (996-1002) and Worcester (1002-16) and Archbishop of York (1002-23) was a noted author of sermons and compiler of laws. Writing under his *nom de plume*, 'the Wolf', he composed this piece around 1014, in the face of renewed Scandinavian attacks, following the flight of King Ethelred II. The annotation is in his own hand and reads 'in addition to far too many other innocent people who have been destroyed all too widely'.

British Library, Cotton MS Nero A.I, f.112.

22   Aldhelm, *De Virginitate*

Early 10th cent.; Winchester (?).

A copy of Aldhelm's (died 709) tract in praise of virginity, dedicated to the nuns of Barking. The initials are reminiscent of earlier Southumbrian forms and the script is partially indebted to Insular half-uncial. The author-portrait sketch was partly redrawn in ink later in the century.

British Library, Royal MS 7.D.XXIV, ff.85v–86.

learning. Such abilities would have been far more widespread within the Church than within lay society, but there are some indications from England, and even more so from the Continent, that tuition could be acquired outside of the Church and that those educated within an ecclesiastical context might re-enter secular society. Also, those from the lower freeborn classes might well gain access to learning through entry into the Church. There is evidence that some specific secular figures, such as the learned king of Northumbria, Aldfrith (686–705), and Alfred the Great (871–99), may well have been able to write as well as to read. Asser writes, of Alfred's youngest son, Aethelweard, that he 'was given over to training in reading and writing under the attentive care of teachers, in company with all the nobly born children of virtually the entire area, and a good many of lesser birth as well'. Conversely, not all clerics were literate, Bede and Alfred both complaining of poor literacy (the former when recounting the problems of training illiterate anglophone priests).

Women also participated in book production. In 735–6 the missionary, Boniface, wrote to Abbess Eadburh of Minster-in-Thanet, requesting that her community '...write for me in gold the epistles of my lord, St Peter the Apostle, to secure honour and reverence for the Holy Scriptures when they are preached before the eyes of the heathen... I send the gold for writing this'. Nuns could obviously produce prestigious work and some fine early correspondence was also composed by them. Aldhelm's work in praise of virginity (22), addressed to the nuns of Barking, demonstrates the prowess at learning that they would have needed to tackle his Joyceian style, and the said ladies responded eagerly to the research task presented by Bede's call for data for his *Ecclesiastical History*. Female religious would also frequently have charge of the care and instruction of children entered early for the religious life. Likewise, the role of mothers in training the young may also occasionally have found a literate expression.

Asser tells us of the young Alfred: 'One day, therefore, when his mother was showing him and his brothers a book of English poetry... she said "I shall give this book to whichever one of you can learn it the fastest." Spurred on by these words, or rather by divine inspiration, and attracted by the beauty of the initial letter in the book, Alfred... immediately took the book from her hand, went to his teacher and learnt it. When it was learnt, he took it back to his mother and recited it.' The wills (*see* 43) of male and female members of the higher, thegnly classes also show that they often owned several books, although it is not possible to say whether they could read them without the aid of a priest.

For the majority of the populace, the nearest they would ever come to handwriting was to glimpse the imposing servicebooks used in religious ceremonies, with the images sometimes explained by the priest if they were lucky, or when attending a court of law, where written evidence became increasingly important from the early 9th century, or where, later, the King's writ (or commands) (*see* 17) might be read out.

Within the monastic community, however, most religious received instruction in the schoolroom, those with any aptitude going on to become *lectors* (scholars) and/or *scriptors* (scribes), a distinction which appears to have been particularly observed in Ireland. Trainee scribes would often be allowed to test their hand, even in prestigious works (such as the Royal Bible (*title-page*) and their efforts, along with corrections by their mentors, may occasionally be detected in passages of the manuscripts themselves. Working practices varied, although in general the order of work consisted of preparation of the parchment (defleshed animal skins), pricking and ruling the layout of the sheets, writing, adding any rubrics (titles, headings etc., generally in *rubeum*, red), decorating, correcting, assembling the sheets into quires (gatherings), sewing together, and binding (perhaps including metalwork covers or a *cumdach*, or shrine). The composition of work teams was variable. For example, in the Lindis-

144, 444

College of St. Francis Library
Joliet, Illinois

25

farne scriptorium, *c.*700, five scribes might work on a school-book whilst great Gospel-books, such as the Lindisfarne Gospels (*see* **18, 51, 55, 65**), were apparently the work of a single artist-scribe. Eadfrith, the alleged maker of the Lindisfarne Gospels, achieved the position of Bishop of Lindisfarne (its binder, Aethilwald, later succeeding him) and was obviously an important member of the community. Perhaps his work on this major cult item represented his own personal *opus dei* and bolstered his position. In Ireland great store was placed upon the 'hero-scribe', and this probably extended to England, although here few references to early scribes (other than the famed Irishman Ultan, celebrated in a poem) survive. Colophons (again favoured primarily by the Irish) preserve the names of some: Wigbald, master-scribe of a large team working on the Barberini Gospels (**10**); and Cutbercht, an Anglo-Saxon working at Salzburg (?) on a Gospel-book which bears his name. Later in the period several 'high-fliers' recorded their work. These included Godeman, probably a Winchester monk and later Abbot of Thorney, whom Bishop Aethelwold commissioned to produce his Benedictional around 971-84, who is commemorated, along with his patron, in a poem (*see* **36, 72**). Aelsinus, perhaps a monk of the New Minster, Winchester, during the second quarter of the 11th century is recorded as the scribe of the Prayerbook of Aelfwine (**23**) and also worked on the New Minster *Liber Vitae* (**15**). But perhaps the most impressive named scribe of them all was a monk of Christ Church, Canterbury, called Eadui Basan. Eadui's work included a Psalter (**24**) and a Gospel-book, both of which are named after him, the Grimbald Gospels and contributions to the York Gospels, the Harley Psalter (*see* **73**) and the earlier Vespasian Psalter (*see* **56, 59**). His work on charters dating from the second and third decades of the 11th century provides a convenient dating reference for his endeavours. The appearance of a common artist, as well as scribe, within certain of these works has led to the suggestion that

23 The Prayerbook of Aelfwine
*c.*1023-35; Winchester, New Minster.

A collection of prayers, Church offices and miscellanea (now in two volumes, Titus D.XXVI-XXVII) written by Aelsinus for Aelfwine (Abbot of the New Minster) whilst he was still a deacon. The miniature depicts an unusual iconography — the Quinity (God the Father, God the Son, the Virgin and Child and the Holy Spirit), derived from the Carolingian Utrecht Psalter. Beneath are Satan, Hades, Judas and the heretic Arius.
British Library, Cotton MS Titus D.XXVII, f.75v.

Eadui may also have been an accomplished artist. It is probably he who is depicted grasping the feet of St Benedict in the Eadui Psalter (**24**).

From the late 9th century onwards patrons were also more readily recorded. Earlier, the works of Bede or of Aldhelm might carry dedications, but the actual owners of books are seldom mentioned. Alfred's 'official publications' allow a number of works to be associated with his circle, the Hatton Pastoral Care (*see* **11**), for example, carrying a prefatory letter of commendation, in the case of this copy addressed to Werferth, Bishop of Worcester. King Athelstan has been shown to have acquired, and commissioned, a number of books, including some from the Continent (**25**) (such as the 'Coronation Gospels' from Lobbes, traditionally used as the oath book at English coronations) and from Ireland (**69**, **12**). He has even been accredited with founding the royal library. King Edgar and his reforming bishops were, predictably, notable patrons (*see* **13**, **14**), and recent scholarship has attempted to extend the generous patronage which Cnut and his wives (*see* **15**) are recorded as displaying to the arts to some of the splendid books produced during the early 11th century. Other secular patrons included St Margaret of Scotland (died 1093), granddaughter of Edmund Ironside, who fled North after the Conquest, resulting in her marriage to King Malcolm III. A pious reformer, Margaret's books included a Gospel-book which contains a poem recording an event in which it was given a quick dip into a river by a careless priest. Another noble lady, Countess Judith of Flanders, owned four Gospel-books written by English scribes (three were made in England and one at St Bertin). Judith was the bride of Tostig Godwinson, the Earl of Northumbria, a major protagonist in the events surrounding the Conquest, and was in England from 1051-64.

In Anglo-Saxon England, therefore, literacy was primarily, if not exclusively, an ecclesiastical preserve. Books would be made within

24 *(overleaf)*   The Eadui Psalter
1012-23; Canterbury, Christ Church.
This imposing Psalter was written by the famous scribe Eadui Basan, who may be depicted here at the feet of St Benedict who bestows the Benedictine Rule upon the adjacent Christ Church monks. Fully painted and tinted drawing styles were often mixed in this fashion.
British Library, Arundel MS 155, f.133.

25 *(overleaf)*   The Athelstan Psalter
English additions of the 10th cent. (pre 939), to a 9th cent. core; Winchester, Old Minster, additions to a book from the Liège area.
King Athelstan (924-39) collected and commissioned a number of books. This manuscript was obtained from the Continent and 'modernized' in accordance with English taste. The additions included this miniature of Christ in Majesty, with heavenly choirs and instruments of the Passion (perhaps emphasising the gift in 926 from Athelstan's brother-in-law Hugh, Duke of the Franks, of a relic of the lance).
British Library, Cotton MS Galba A.XVIII, f.2v.

religious communities for a variety of patrons: for the community itself, or for another religious establishment; for priests, all of whom required books to perform their duties; for individual ecclesiastics, often of high rank; and for secular figures, male and female, royal or noble.

Such were the makers and audiences of Anglo-Saxon manuscripts: it remains to outline the scope of material which was encompassed by their tastes.

The range of works copied or composed in Anglo-Saxon England reveals a culture indebted to the learning of Antiquity, the Early Christian world, the Continent and eastern Christendom. Works by Pliny, Cicero (26), Dioscorides (*see* 29) and Vitruvius might be found within English libraries, along with those of Augustine, Gregory the Great (*see* 11), Ephrem the Syrian and other Church Fathers and of important Christian scholars and poets, such as Orosius (27), Isidore of Seville (71), Sedulius and Prudentius (28).

Inspired by such a legacy many new works were created. Bede explored the nature of time and the natural world, and created an influential brand of historiography (*see* 9) out of a tradition of the annalistic recording of events and of semi-historical polemic. Byrhtferth of Ramsey later continued to advance the frontiers of scientific knowledge, in the Bedan tradition, whilst aspects of Anglo-Saxon medicinal knowledge (culled both from Antiquity and from herbal and folk remedies, the latter often of a decidedly magical character) were preserved in the Leechbooks (*see* **29, 30**). Astronomical, astrological and calendrical information were also an important part of world knowledge for the Anglo-Saxons and their contemporaries and a number of works contain information upon these subjects (*see* **26, 32, 74**). An interest in geography was also manifested in copies of texts such as the *Marvels of the East* (**31**), descriptions of the Holy Land and travellers tales, such as that recounted to Alfred the Great by the Norseman, Ohthere. An

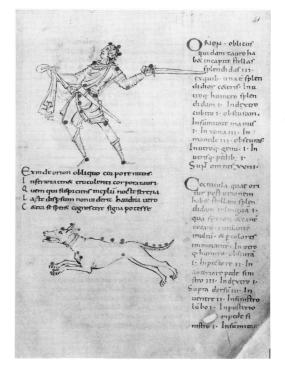

26 Cicero, *Aratea*
Late 10th cent.; Fleury (?).

Cicero's Latin verse translation of the *Phaenomena* of the Greek philosopher Aratus. An important astronomical treatise, essential to early medieval computus (calculation of time). The personifications of the constellations (here Orion and his hound) incorporate the stars as orange dots. They were probably copied from a Carolingian model by an English artist working on the Continent. The text was also known and copied in England.
British Library, Harley MS 2506, f.41.

27　The Old English Orosius

10th cent., second quarter; Winchester.

An early copy of the Alfredian English translation of the *Universal Histories Against the Pagans*, composed in the early 5th century by the Spaniard Paulus Orosius. Presenting, as it does, the history of a Christian society beleaguered by paganism, it was a suitable choice for inclusion in Alfred's programme. It is often termed the Tollemache or Helmingham Orosius after later ownership. The initial is of Wormald's 'Type I' and the script is an early square minuscule.

British Library, Add. MS 47967, f.5v.

28　Prudentius, *Psychomachia*

Late 10th cent.; southern England.

Luxuria tempting men to abandon their arms in favour of debauchery, from a cycle of illustrations to the *Spiritual Combat* by the Spaniard Prudentius (348–*c*.410). The *Psychomachia* is an allegorical poem on the conflict between Christianity and paganism, symbolized by a struggle between the virtues and vices.

British Library, Add. MS 24199, f.18.

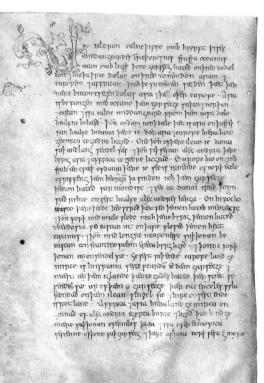

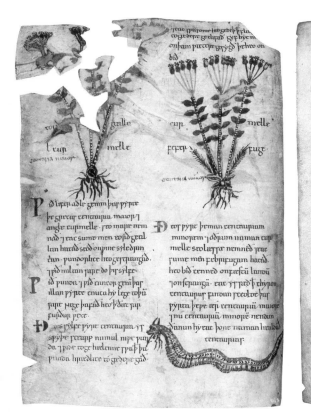

29 *(left)*   The *Herbarium* of Apuleius Platonicus
Early 11th cent.; Canterbury, Christ Church.

Feverfew and its uses (including remedies for poison, symbolized by the viper), from a cycle of herbal illustrations inherited from Antiquity. Herbalism, or wort-cunning, lay at the root of Anglo-Saxon medicine, along with astronomy, astrology, prayers, charms and magic. Several relevant works were known from Antiquity and this volume also includes texts by Dioscorides and Sextus Placitus.

British Library, Cotton MS Vitellius C.III, f.32v.

30 *(right above)*   Bald's Leechbook
Mid-10th cent.; Winchester.

One of several leech, or physician's, handbooks. A colophon records ownership by one, Bald. These treatises are anthologies of herbal and magical remedies, charms and prayers. This folio carries an amulet 'Against every evil rune lay, and one full of elvish tricks, write for the bewitched man this writing in Greek letters: alpha, omega, iesum [?] beronikh. Again, another dust or powder and drink against a rune lay; take a bramble apple, and lupins, and

pulegium, pound them, then sift them, put them in a pouch, lay them under the altar, sing nine masses over them, put the dust into milk, drip thrice some holy water upon them, administer this to drink at three hours...'

British Library, Royal MS 12.D.XVII, f.52v.

31 *(opposite)*   Marvels of the East
11th cent., second quarter; Winchester or Canterbury (?)

The fabulous inhabitants of the East (including an elephant), illustrating a Late Antique treatise copied in this miscellaneous volume of world knowledge. The bilingual text is written in an English caroline minuscule (Latin) and an Anglo-Saxon round minuscule (Old English).

British Library, Cotton MS Tiberius B.V (pt I), f.81.

Nascuntur & ibi homines habentes statura
pedū·xv· corp̄ habentes candidū duas in
una habentes capite facies rubra genua naso
longo capillis nigris·cū temp̄ gignendi fuerit
suis manib; transferunt in indiam & ibi
plem reddunt :

ær beoð akende men ða beoð fiftyne fota
lange ⁊hi habbað hƿit lic ⁊tƿegen ꝑ anum
hearde bið ⁊ an ƿide ƿead ⁊lange noꞅu
ſƿeaꞃt feax þon hi kennan ƿillað hꝺ ƿaꝺ
hi to indeum ⁊hyꞃa ge cynd oꞃ yeoꞃold
bꞃingað :

tem liconia in gallia nascū̄tur homines tripato
colore quorum capita capita leonum pedib;
xx·ore amplissimo sic uannum hominē cū
cognouerūt aut siqs ꝓsequatur longe fugiūt
& sanguine sudat hi putant homines fuisse :

liconia in gallia hatte þland þær beoð ꝺnenig
acennað ꝺ ꝓ fellicer hyer bona heorða beoð
gemona ⁊ꝑa leona hearðo ⁊hi beoð tƿentiger
fota lange ⁊hi habbað micelne mūð ⁊ꝑa
fann gifth hƿylcne man ondam landum on
gꞃað oððe him hƿyle follizende bið þon
ꞃeoꞃƿað hi ⁊ꞃleoð ⁊blode þ hi ſƿætað
þaꞃ beoð menn ge ꝑenede :

R. Cotton Bruce

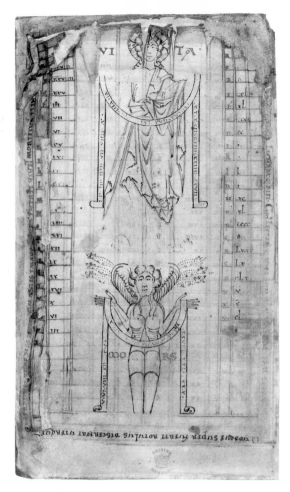

32 The Tiberius Psalter

*c.*1050; Winchester.

Diagram from computistical material preceding the Psalter, depicting Christ / Vita (Life) and Mors (Death) holding scrolls with numbers for calculating the chances of recovery or death. Computus (calculation of time) was essential to the reckoning of the ecclesiastical year and was often inter-woven with astrological / astronomical and medical lore.

British Library, Cotton MS Tiberius C.VI, f.6v.

33 *Mappa Mundi*

11th cent., second quarter; Winchester or Canterbury (?).

A world map, depicting Britain in the lower left-hand corner and Jerusalem at the centre, incorporated into a miscellaneous volume of world knowledge. It prefaces the *Periegesis of Priscian* but is unrelated to it. It illustrates the advanced state of Anglo-Saxon cartography, culled from Antiquity and from a long tradition of pilgrimage and travel.

British Library, Cotton MS Tiberius B.V (pt I), f.56v.

advanced and intriguing world map also survives in an early 11th-century English manuscript, prefiguring the later medieval *mappae mundi* (33).

A 10th-century trend towards the production of anthologies also led to the recording of a rich poetic tradition (*see* 38), many examples of which were originally composed for the mead hall and preserved orally. In addition to secular poems such as *The Wanderer* (*see* 38), *The Wife's Lament* and *Wulf*, and epics such as *Beowulf* (37) and *The Battle of Maldon* a number of moving Christian poems were composed, such as *Caedmon's Hymn*, *The Dream of the Rood*

and *Judith*. Rules of metre governing Greek and Latin verse were also brought to bear upon Anglo-Saxon poetic composition, largely through the agency of the Canterbury school under Archbishop Theodore and Abbot Hadrian, and its pupils, notably Aldhelm. The *Riddles* composed by authors such as Aldhelm and Tatwine, although often amusing, were designed to assist in the propagation of such rules (*see* 34).

Various books were required for the performance of worship. The Scriptures were available in several types of manuscripts: Bibles (*see title-page*, 49, 57), Gospel–books (*see* 1, 5, 7, 10, 48,

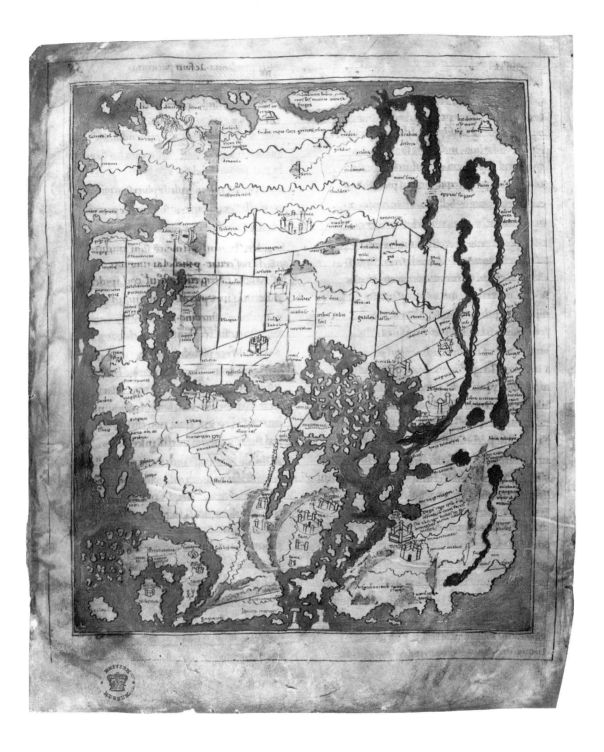

Terra dicta a superiori parte qua teritur. Humus ab inferiori uel humus
terra ū sub magis. Tellus aute qua fructus ei tollimus. hec et ops dicta eoq sese
opem fructibus eadem & aquis abquerendo et colendo uocatur. proprie
aut terra ad distinctionem harene. Arida nuncupatur sic scriptura A:
porro uocauit ds Aridam terram; ;

QVATERNIS QVOQVE VERSIBVS CONTEXTA QVAE GRE

CA LINGVA TETRASTICA DICVNTVR VT AIT

DE TERRA INCIPIVNT ENIGMATA · 84

ALTRIX CVNCTORV

i. homines cunctos.   i. portat
QVOS MVNDVS GESTAT IN ORBE

i. uocor
Nuncupor · et merito quia numquam pignora tantu

Improba sic lacerant maternas dente papillas

Prole uirens aestate tabescens tempore brumae;

DE VENTO
i. homines
Cernere me nulli possunt nec prendere palmis

Arguitum uocis crepitu cito pando per orbem

Viribus horrisonis ualeo confringere quercas

Nam superos ego pulso polos et rura peragro;

DE NVBE
Versicolor fugiens caelum terramque profundam

Non tellure locus mihi nec in parte polorū est.

Exilium nullus modo tam crudele ueretur
Quia qui exilium patit in eo loco uno in quo tu ne est maret & ego uero in mundū discurro;

X Pignus pignoris i.
filius uel soboles.
Pignus pigneris i.
uadimonium;
Quomodo lacerunt
filios meos t habi-
tatores meos cu
alis hoc nonfaci
unte matribus
suis;

Bruma abreui
mori ds solis;

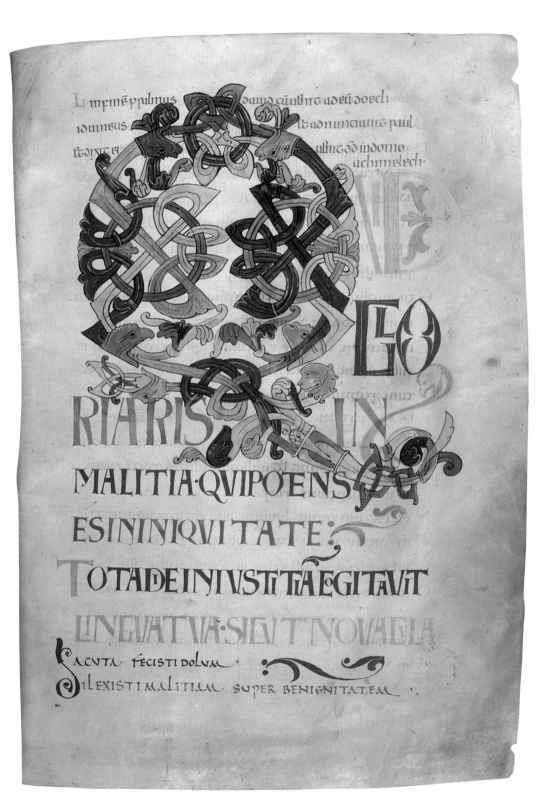

In finē ppsalmus dauid cū ūthit adeū doech idumeus. & adnūnciauit paul & dixit ei uthit qd indomo achimelech.

QUID GLORIARIS IN MALITIA QUI POENS ES IN INIQUITATE TOTA DIE INIUSTITIA EGITAVIT LINGUA TUA SICUT NOVACLA

ACUTA FECISTI DOLUM ·
DILEXISTI MALITIAM SUPER BENIGNITATEM ·

34 *(page 36)*   Aldhelm's *Riddles*
10th cent., second half; Canterbury, Christ Church.

Riddles, often of an amusing character, were very popular in England and were composed by the early Canterbury school and its pupils, notably Aldhelm (died 709) and Tatwine, to instruct in poetic metre. The initial is of Wormald's 'Type IIb'.

This folio includes the following items, exhibiting even *c.*700 a concern with 'green' issues:

'On the Earth
The nursemaid of all creatures born by the world on its orb
I am called: and rightly so, because never do wicked children
Thus lacerate their mother's breast with their teeth.
I grow green with fruit in the Summer: I decay in the Winter.
On a cloud
Multicoloured in hue, I flee the sky and the deep earth;
There is no place for me on the ground nor in any part of the poles
No one fears an exile as cruel as mine,
But I make the world grow green with my rainy tears.'
British Library, Royal MS 12.C.XXIII, f.84.

35 *(page 37)*   The Bosworth Psalter
Late 10th cent.; south-eastern England (Christ Church, Canterbury ?).

The text of this servicebook is expressly adapted for use in the Benedictine Office. It has a calendar added between 988 and 1012 with a Canterbury and Glastonbury flavour. Ownership by St Dunstan (died 988) has been suggested, but remains unproven.
British Library, Add. MS 37517, f.33.

36   The Benedictional of St Aethelwold
971-84; Winchester, Old Minster.

Miniature from Bishop Aethelwold's book of episcopal blessings, depicting a servicebook in use at the dedication of a church. Fully painted and tinted drawing techniques were often combined in this manner.
British Library, Add. MS 49598, f.118v.

53, 60-69) or lectionaries, groups of Old Testament books **(54)**, and Psalters (*see* **24, 25, 32, 35, 59, 73, 75**). Missals and breviaries (or their components) were required to perform the mass and the divine office, respectively (although the less lavish copies of these seldom survive). A few choirbooks still exist (*see* **74, 77**), along with some specific servicebooks, such as the benedictionals containing episcopal blessings (*see* **36, 72**). The English, along with the Irish, were also much given to exegetical, or interpretative, writing and commentary upon the Scriptures, Bede and Alcuin being major exponents of this art. Homilies and sermons were also a strength, with Aelfric and Wulfstan excelling in this sort of composition during the late 10th century (*see* **20, 21**). A rich tradition of private devotion also existed, represented primarily by a group of early 9th-century Mercian prayerbooks and by later anthologies (*see* **23, 39-42**).

With such an impressive ecclesiastical tradition it is not surprising that Anglo-Saxon England should have generated a number of local saints' lives, in addition to producing copies of

beneath the heavens, rulers in the hall,
cannot say who received that cargo.'

British Library, Cotton MS Vitellius A.XV (pt II), f.133.

38 The Exeter Book

10th cent., second half; south-western England.

The Exeter Book is an important anthology of Anglo-Saxon vernacular poetry (as is the Vercelli Codex), some of which was composed much earlier. This folio shows the end of *The Wanderer* and the beginning of *The Gifts of Men*. The script is a square minuscule.

The end of *The Wanderer* includes this passage on the desolation and loneliness of the lordless man :
    'Nothing is ever easy in the kingdom of earth,
    the world beneath the heavens is in the hands of fate;
    Here possessions are fleeting, here friends are fleeting
    here man is fleeting, here kinsman is fleeting,
    the whole world becomes a wilderness...'

Exeter, Cathedral Library, MS 3501, f.78.

37 Beowulf

*c.*1000

This sole manuscript of *Beowulf* was damaged by fire in 1731. Date and place of composition remain hotly disputed. Although 'Christianized' it tells of a pagan Germanic (Scandinavian) past, of the conflict between good and evil. Some view it as having been composed in Cnut's reign, but the consensus places it in the 7th century or thereabouts, citing archaeological parallels (such as Sutton Hoo). It was probably copied as part of an 'anthology', but may well have had a background of oral recitation.

This folio carries the end of a passage describing a ship burial:
    'Then high above his head they placed
    a golden banner and let the waves bear him,
    bequeathed him to the sea; their hearts were grieving,
    their minds mourning. Mighty men

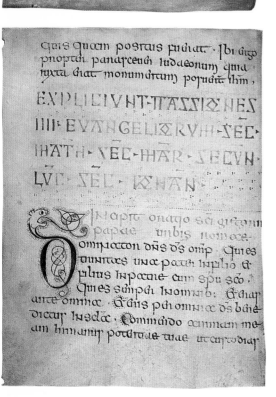

more 'universal' hagiographical works. Bede's lives of St Cuthbert (*see* **12**), Felix's *Life of St Guthlac* and lives of Swithin and Alphege are among the English contributions to the genre.

A secular biographical tradition also emerged, perhaps under Carolingian influence, manifested in Asser's *Life of Alfred*, the Life of

39   The Royal Prayerbook
Early 9th cent.; Mercia (Worcester ?).

One of a group of Mercian prayerbooks whose texts are compiled around a central theme, in this case Christ as the healer of mankind. It has been suggested that it was owned by a physician, possibly a woman. The script is a set minuscule.

British Library, Royal MS 2.A.XX, f.17.

40   The Book of Nunnaminster
Early 9th cent.; Mercia.

End of Gospel extracts and beginning of a prayer attributed to Gregory the Great, from one of a group of Mercian prayerbooks, this one focusing upon the life of Christ. The mixed display capitals are ultimately of Northumbrian inspiration (note the use of the Greek character for **P** in *Passiones*, Greek interpolations often occur in Insular manuscripts). Script is a set minuscule, tending towards hybrid minuscule.

British Library, Harley MS 2965, f.16v.

42 *(opposite)*   The Book of Cerne
*c.*820–40; Mercia (Lichfield ?).

The most imposing of a group of Mercian prayerbooks arranged around a theme (in this case primarily the Communion of Saints) for use in private devotions. The compilation fuses material drawn largely from two devotional traditions: Roman and Celtic. This opening introduces the Passion narrative from St John's Gospel. The initial **h** and display panel incorporate a whimsical zoomorphic vocabulary (related to 'Trewhiddle style' metalwork) and the evangelist miniature is unusual in placing full-length symbol beneath human bust, perhaps reflecting contemporary liturgical use when explaining the meaning of the evangelists and their symbols. The script is a cursive minuscule.

Cambridge, University Library, MS Ll.1.10, ff.31v–32.

41 The Book of Nunnaminster

Early 9th cent.; Mercia.

Prayer against poor eyesight, from a Mercian prayerbook. It is followed by an Old English record (in pointed minuscule script) of property given to the nunnery at Winchester (Nunnaminster) by its founder, Ealhswith (died 909), wife of Alfred the Great. Herself a Mercian, it has been suggested that this book may have belonged to Ealhswith at some point and have been bequeathed to the Nunnaminster along with other of her possessions, although this attractive theory cannot be proven.

British Library, Harley MS 2965, f.40v.

43 The Will of Atheling Athelstan

*c.*1014; ?

Several wills survive, of both men and women. Athelstan was the eldest son of Ethelred II ('Unraed') and his household, possessions and relationships may be glimpsed through his bequests. These include: to his brother, Edmund Ironside, 'the sword which belonged to King Offa'; to Godwine the Driveller 'the three hides at Ludgershall'; 'to Aelfnoth my sword-polisher the notched [?] inlaid sword, and to my staghuntsman the stud which is on Coleridge'; to the church where he was to be buried, numerous gifts including 'the drinking-horn which I have bought from the community at the Old Minster'; to his foster-mother, Aelfswith, 'because of her great deserts, the estate at Weston, which I bought from my father for 250 mancuses of gold, by weight'.

The opening of the document is in one hand and the body of the will in another, perhaps indicating some lapse in time. It is a cyrograph in form, i.e. two copies were severed through the line of the word *cyrographum* which, when put together, would authenticate both copies.

British Library, Stowe Charter 37.

Edward the Confessor and the notorious 'Apology' or *Encomium* of his mother, Emma (*see* 16). The importance of lineage and kinship within Anglo-Saxon society and kingship is also displayed in the genealogies which were composed, tracing descent from figures such as Woden (and thereby often to biblical figures), to establish the worthiness and legitimacy of various individuals and their houses. The possibilities presented by the foregoing works for use as propaganda do not appear to have been overlooked, and nor (eventually) was that of another major work, the *Anglo-Saxon Chronicle* (*see* 44), commenced during Alfred's reign and continued in a number of versions, one extending to 1154.

Alongside the production of these many and varied books was a tradition of pragmatic literacy represented by the charters (property documents), the records of ecclesiastical synods and councils (*see* 8), manumissions (*see* 45), the royal writs (*see* 17) and major administrative records, such as the *Tribal* and *Burghal Hidages*. A number of wills (of both men and women) also survive (*see* **43**), including that of Alfred the Great, and, along with the charters, provide an insight into property ownership. A rare survival of an estate document relating to the possessions of Ely gives a glimpse into the rural economy (**46**), whilst documents relating to trade and to guild regulations shed light upon urban life. Perhaps most important of all are the law-codes issued by rulers such as Ine of Wessex (**47**), Ethelbert of Kent and Alfred which furnish probably the most detailed and stimulating insight into life in Anglo-Saxon England.

44 The Anglo-Saxon Chronicle
Mid-11th cent.; Abingdon.

The *Chronicle* (a series of annals, or yearly entries of events) was probably 'published' around 890-2 and reflects the interests of King Alfred, even if it was not composed in his immediate circle. Its potential as propaganda was certainly recognized subsequently. Seven copies survive and were continued in various centres. An essentially West Saxon view of the history of the English is given, although this version (known as 'C' or the 'Abingdon Chronicle') incorporates a rare survival of Mercian annals (the *Mercian Register*). These entries (916-24) emphasise the role of Alfred's daughter, Aethelflaed, Lady of the Mercians, in reconquering the Danelaw and the deposition of her daughter, Aelfwyn, following her death. There could be no rival claim to the emergent national unity and its West Saxon monarchy !

British Library, Cotton MS Tiberius B.I, f.140v.

45 Manumission
Added *c.*925 to an early-8th-cent. Gospel-book; originally Northumbria, addition perhaps made at Canterbury (?).

The earliest extant English manumission (grant of release from slavery). It reads 'King Athelstan freed Eadhelm immediately after he first became king. Aelfheah the mass-priest and the community, Aelfric the reeve, Wulfnoth the White... were witness... He who averts this - may have the disfavour of God and of all the relics which I, by God's mercy, have obtained in England. And I grant the children the same that I grant the father'. Documents were occasionally written into liturgical volumes, presumably to bestow added authority upon them.

British Library, Royal MS 1.B.VII, f.15v.

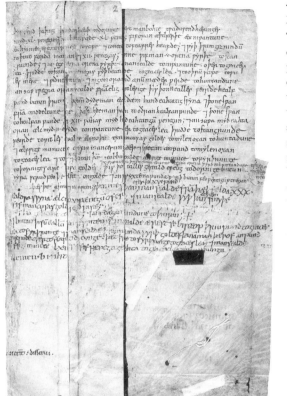

47   The Laws of Ine of Wessex

Mid-10th century; Winchester

The law-code of Ine, King of Wessex (688–*c.*726), was drawn up some time between 688 and 694. It is preserved here in the 'Parker Chronicle' (the earliest copy of the Anglo-Saxon Chronicle) as a supplement to the laws of Alfred, who drew upon it. These, and the laws of several 7th-century rulers of Kent, provide a valuable insight into the everyday lives and social structures of the early English, in which legal status of individuals and their misdemeanours were determined by worth, as defined by the *wergild* (blood-money or compensation-money). This folio includes the following laws:

'If a husband (*ceorl* or freeman) and wife have a child together and the husband dies, the mother is to have her child and rear it; she is to be given six shillings for its maintenance, a cow in summer, an ox in winter, the kinsmen are to take charge of the paternal home, until the child is grown up.

If anyone goes away from his lord without permission, or steals into another 'shire', and is discovered there, he is to return to where he was before and pay sixty shillings to his lord.

Cambridge, Corpus Christi College, MS 173, f.49v.

46   Ely Abbey Farming Memoranda

*c.*1007-25; Ely.

A very rare survival of an informal document relating to rural estate management. The memoranda consist of a list and valuation of livestock, seed, implements, ships etc. supplied by Ely to Thorney Abbey, an inventory of livestock and a list of fenland rents (payable in eels). They were written by four hands over a period of time, probably as working notes.

British Library, Add. MS 61735.

Materials and techniques

The sheets of parchment or vellum (the former technically sheep or goatskin and the latter calf, with parchment the better generic term) would be defleshed in a bath of alum and lime, stretched, scraped, perhaps whitened, trimmed, pricked and ruled, adorned with script and decoration and arranged in gatherings (quires), unless they were single sheet documents, and then bound into the book or codex form. The technical method of book manufacture (codicology) again shows that, during the early period, Insular scriptoria formulated their own responses to late Antique practice, which differed in many respects from Continental techniques. Insular membrane is often thick and suede-like or stiff and 'celluloid', exhibiting little contrast between hair and flesh sides (unlike its thinner Antique and Continental counterparts which have a marked contrast, with hair follicles often speckling the yellower hair sides). Insular quire arrangement therefore had no need to place the double sheets (bifolia) in such a manner that, when folded, like would face like at an opening, in Continental fashion. Hair sides tend to face outwards, with hair facing flesh at an opening. Quires were generally of 10s or 8s (5 or 4 double sheets, or bifolia, folded into booklets), 8s becoming the norm in England following the reforms and heightened Mediterranean influence of *c*.700. Although one bifolium would be written on at a time (the text not, therefore, being continuous, and consideration having had to be devoted to layout ahead of time) the sheets were arranged in gatherings prior to writing and were pricked (in all four margins) and ruled with a hard point, to guide the writing lines, from the outside of the quire after it had been folded. On the Continent, bifolia would be pricked in their outer margins only and ruled straight across, prior to folding. Membrane was costly and only the Irish occasionally dispensed with ruling in their pocket Gospel-books (*see* **69**) where the text block was so condensed that it virtually guided itself. The number of skins used varied in accordance with the character and size of the book. For the Lindisfarne Gospels, a large and luxurious work, no fewer than 127 calf-skins were required (*see* **62**).

Occasionally experiments with Continental techniques occurred, notably in an Hiberno-Saxon milieu during the 7th century, at Canterbury during the first half of the 9th century and in Wessex during the early 10th century, all areas where, historically, heightened Continental influence might be expected. With the advent in England of caroline minuscule from the mid-10th century, Continental methods of preparation were also generally adopted (although Insular symptoms persisted, such as hair sides forming the outside of quires).

The assembled quires would then be sewn together and bound. They were generally sewn onto a number of leather (alum tawed) cords, the ends of which were then threaded through holes and channels drilled into thick wooden boards (preferably oak or another hardwood, to deter worms) and secured with wooden dowels. Endbands would be sewn to the ends of the spine to further consolidate the binding and the boards and spine would be covered with damp leather which might be moulded over a raised design (*see* **48**), tooled with a pattern, and/or adorned with metal fittings. Cords might also serve to tie the boards together at the foredges, pressure preventing the membrane from returning to the shape of the animal. Very few such early bindings have survived, although two 8th-century examples associated with St Boniface remain, and pictorial sources (*see* **68**) supplement the knowledge which may be gleaned from an 'archaeological' examination of traces within the books themselves, many of which were rebound later. A remarkable early survival of an Anglo-Saxon binding is the Gospel of St John (**48**) which was probably given as a gift to the shrine of St Cuthbert by the Wearmouth/Jarrow communities, *c*.698. Fascinatingly, the binding technique differs from that described above, in that the quires are sewn together with thread using two needles, rather than being sewn onto supports – a

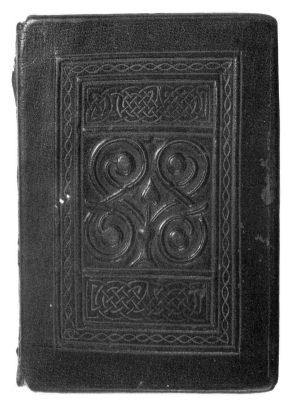

48　The Stonyhurst or Cuthbert Gospel
Late 7th cent.; Wearmouth / Jarrow.

This small copy of St John's Gospel, written in a fine uncial script, was probably presented for inclusion in the coffin of St Cuthbert (died 687, relics translated 698). It possesses a rare contemporary binding of decorated leather over wooden boards. The sewing technique attaching the quires and boards is unusual within the West and is paralleled in Coptic sewing (from Christian Egypt), rendering it a tangible example of direct eastern influence.

British Library, Loan MS 74, front cover.

CODICIBVS SACRIS HOSTILI CLADE PERVSTIS
ESDRA DŌ FERVENS HOC REPARAVIT OPVS

49 The Codex Amiatinus

Late 7th cent.(?), pre 716; Wearmouth / Jarrow.

The scribe Ezra (adapted from an Italian Cassiodoran model) from one of the three great Bibles which Bede tells us were made for Ceolfrith, Abbot of Wearmouth / Jarrow. This copy was intended for presentation to the Pope by Ceolfrith who set out for Rome in 716. He died *en route* and his dedication inscription was later doctored in favour of its new home at Monte Amiato. So classicizing is it in style that it was only recently identified as Anglo-Saxon, rather than made by Mediterranean craftsmen.

Florence, Biblioteca Medicea–Laurenziana, MS Amiatino 1, f.V.

50 Writing tablet and styli

Late 7th - early 8th cent.; Northumbria (styli), Suffolk (tablet).

The elaborately carved bone tablet, found at Blythburgh, was recessed to receive a waxen writing surface on its reverse (it may have carried runic script at some point). The styli, for inscribing in the wax, are of copper alloy or bone and were excavated at Whitby.

British Museum, Dept. of Medieval and Later Antiquities.

technique practised in Coptic Egypt.

In addition to the codex (book) form, wax tablets were inherited from Antiquity (continuing in use almost to the present century). Wooden boards, sometimes in sets bound together with leather thongs, would be hollowed out to receive wax which was written upon with a metal or bone point (stylus), which often had a triangular end used for erasure. These were reusable and could serve for drafting, teaching or even as 'exotic', formal items. Two Insular examples of tablets survive, along with numerous styli (*see* **2, 50**).

An early predilection for a 'tricolor' of pigments consisting of red (red lead), green (verdigris – a copper sulphate) and yellow (orpiment – a trisulphide of arsenic) gave way to a more extensive palette with the growth of Mediterranean influence, seen in the Codex Amiatinus (**49**) and the Lindisfarne Gospels (*see* **18, 65**), *c.*700. This incorporated mineral (e.g. malachite

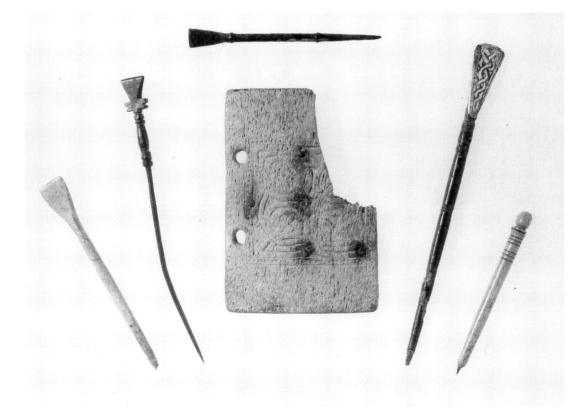

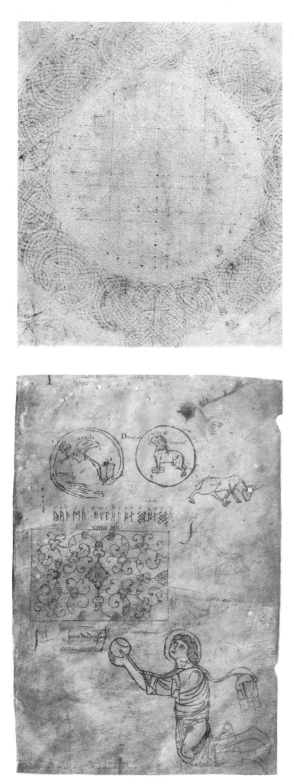

and azurite), plant (e.g. woad and turnsole) and animal (e.g. kermes, an insect dye) extracts which would be mixed with clarified egg-white (*clarea*) as the essential binding medium (although additives ranging from stale urine to ear wax are known to have been used during the Middle Ages to achieve the desired coloristic effect). In addition to local substances, exotic pigments such as cinnabar and ultramarine (made from lapis lazuli, at that period almost

51 *(left above)* The Lindisfarne Gospels
*c.*700; Lindisfarne.

Construction marks to guide layout on the back of one of the carpet pages. Prickings guide the interlace, but much of the detail was executed free-hand. The geometric rules governing the essential structure of Insular ornament may be clearly perceived here. Dividers, compasses, rulers and pricking tools might be used in setting out such designs.
British Library, Cotton MS Nero D.IV, f.94 (detail).

52 *(left below)* The Tollemache or Helmingham Orosius
Additions of the second half of the 10th cent. and later to a book of the second quarter of the 10th cent.; Winchester.

These drawings were added to the fly-leaves of a copy of the Alfredian translation into English of Orosius's *Histories Against the Pagans* (*see* **27**). They depict evangelist symbols, an angel, a vine-scroll and a series of runes and their alphabetic equivalents, with inscriptions by a 16th-century owner. Spare parchment was often used to try out designs, as were stone, slate, bone and other cheaper materials.
British Library, Add. MS 47967, f.1.

53 *(right)* Gospel-book
Early 8th cent.; Northumbria.

One of the Eusebian canon tables (a Gospel concordance system devised by Eusebius of Caesarea during the 4th century) from a Gospel-book which exhibits influence in its script from the Lindisfarne scriptorium, although its decoration is rather conservative. The scope of the decoration of what was probably a working servicebook contrasts with the elaboration of a cult object such as the Lindisfarne Gospels (*see* **18, 65**).
British Library, Royal MS 1.B.VII, f.10v.

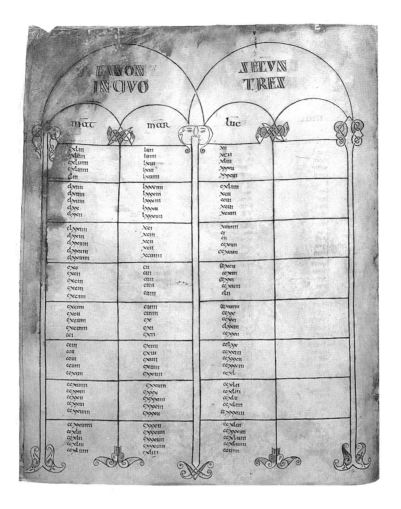

exclusively available from Persia) occur, finding their way even to the island of Lindisfarne. Gold leaf could be used, laid on gum or fish-glue, burnished or unburnished, or gold could be powdered to form an even more costly ink or paint. Mixing and layering of pigments extended the range still further (techniques seen at their extremes in the Book of Kells) (*see* **61, 62**). From the 10th century the use of colour changes somewhat, although the pigments remain essentially the same (even until the 14th century): tinted drawing used thin washes of colour, or coloured outlines, whilst full-paint-ing used thicker pigments and would often give substance and opacity to the colours by adding white lead (*see* **24**). Any drawing (*see* **52**) and layout was generally executed in ink or with a hard metal point (*see* **54**), with a lead point (leaving marks resembling a pencil) sometimes being used from *c*.1000. A chalk-like substance also occurs and compasses and dividers were often used to assist layout (*see* **51**). Ink generally consisted of oak-gall mixed with carbon (lamp-black) and/or iron extract. Quill pens and brushes were both used and a knife was sometimes employed for erasure.

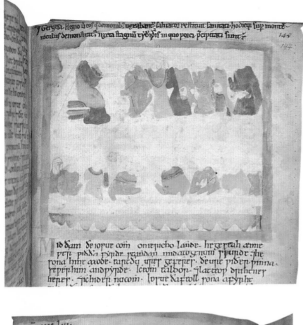

54   The Old English Illustrated Hexateuch

11th cent., second quarter; Canterbury, St Augustine's.

This Old English translation of the first six books of the Old Testament (largely by the homilist Aelfric, with later additions possibly by Byrhtferth of Ramsey) contains an extensive cycle of illustrations, of probable Late Antique or Byzantine inspiration. These miniatures show the stages of execution, from metal-point drawing and under-painting to definition in ink, in a mixture of fully painted and tinted drawing.

British Library, Cotton MS Claudius B.IV, ff.144, 92v and 63v.

Soþlice hi ledon forð heora lac ongean þæt iosep inrode. 7 rollon on þa eorþan. 7 ge eaðmeddon wiþ hine. Iosep hi on cneowða axsode lice. 7 axode hi, hwæþer heora fæder þære hal þe lihim þore fæder oþþe hwæþer he leofode. þa cwædon hi gerund irþin þeow uþ fæder gyt he leofaþ. Ða iosep geseah hir ge medde dan broþor benIamin, þa cwæþ he. Is þis eower gingra broþor rodon, 7 þe he cwæþ god gemil rige þe runu min. 7 he wearð 7 wearð wiðe, 7 for ȝiod þæt him rollon ana for hir broþor þingon. 7 he eode into hir bed cleofan 7 weop. þa he hæt ge þwæ, þa eode he ut to him 7 hi æton. On fundon, þar gy þwæron hit nær na alifed þæt hi æt gæd ir æton. 7 hi man oxs þid þence.

onfundon þa þa
Ebreiscan.

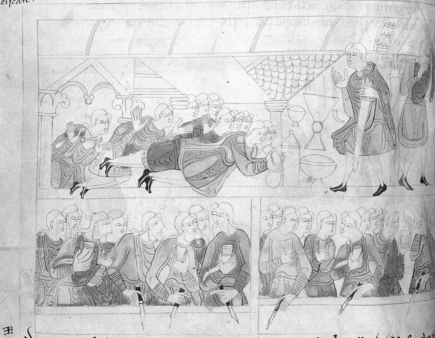

idioma lingue hebree ē: ut ebetate p̄ sanietate ponat sicut ibi. In stillicidiis suis inebriata
germinabit: haud dubium quin terra plurimis irrigata.

Abead iosep his gerefan. 7 cwæþ fille heora saccas mid hwæte swa hi berun magon 7 lege heora ælcer feoh on hir agenne sæc. 7 min minne sylfrenan læfel 7 þær hwætes wurð þe he ealde 7 do on þæs gyngestan sæc. 7 he dyde swa.

p̄ sacculo persone ul' rollen habet in hebreo. p̄ condi. i. poculo. quod etiam in ysaia legitur. Aquila
hum. Symmachus scalam transtulerunt.

Script

Limited Anglo-Saxon acquaintance with script prior to the conversion is indicated by Germanic runes (*see* **52**), an angular alphabet, suited for carving, thought to have derived from a southern European alphabet (perhaps Latin or northern Italic). Their use was, however, restricted to short inscriptions, often of a talismanic nature. The Celts also possessed a script of similar derivation, ogham, which was again of a limited, élitist and talismanic character and which consisted of linear strokes placed in relation to a central line.

The earliest extant examples of Insular, Latin, script date to the late 6th–early 7th century (the Springmount Bog Tablets (**2**) and Codex Usserianus Primus) and are from Ireland. Their script seems to be descended from the personal bookhand of the educated man of late Antiquity ('literary cursive', sometimes called 'cursive half-uncial' or 'quarter-uncial'). This is in keeping with the way in which Ireland was introduced to literacy: late and via the Church. Its early script was therefore initially free of the excesses of the lower grade business hands of the Roman Empire ('old' and 'new Roman cursive') and their vulgarized derivatives, and also of the more formal book hands ('square capitals', 'rustic capitals', 'uncials' and 'half-uncials'), although the latter exerted an influence upon developments during the 7th century.

Working from this middle-grade base, script developed (as is its wont) formal and informal expressions, suited to different purposes. The 7th century witnessed attempts to upgrade the Insular hands, producing something approaching the half-uncials of Antiquity ('early Insular half-uncial'), with hybrid variants, and to downgrade them to form more cursive (rapid and more easily written) minuscule scripts. This evolutionary phase has been termed 'Phase I' by T.J. Brown. It encompassed the 7th and early 8th centuries (continuing in Ireland alongside subsequent developments) and comprised formal half-uncial/hybrid minuscule scripts (as seen in the Book of Durrow) (*see also* **19**) and three types of minuscule: Irish; Type A –

Northumbrian Phase I minuscule (heavy, compressed, and pointed - seen in the Vatican Paulinus); Type B - Southumbrian Phase I minuscule (lighter, less compressed, and often more cursively written - seen in the handwriting of St Boniface) (*see* **19**).

This phase was expanded to produce a complete hierarchy of scripts - 'Phase II' - from the late 7th to 9th centuries. This included majuscule scripts (generally bilinear and formally written with a broad, straight pen, with frequent pen-lifts), notably Insular half-uncials (one of the most characteristic and influential Insular scripts, which achieved its distinctive, fully developed form in the Lindisfarne scriptorium, *c.*700 – *see* the Lindisfarne Gospels (**55**)). This canonical half-uncial script was probably influenced by Antique scripts, which became increasingly popular within romanizing centres, such as Canterbury and Wearmouth/ Jarrow, where uncials (a stately, rounded script, criticized by St Jerome for its excesses, which could lead to letters an 'inch high', or 'uncial') were used for works such as the three Bibles commissioned by Abbot Ceolfrith (*see* **57**) and the Vespasian Psalter (**56, 59**). Uncials and rustic capitals were also used in a limited fashion for display purposes (titles etc.), and a distinctive Hiberno-Saxon display script composed of angular capitals (perhaps influenced by epigraphy), rune-like forms and uncials or half-uncials was popularized by the Lindisfarne scriptorium (**65**). Within Phase II minuscules (quattrolinear, 'lower-case' scripts, written with a slanted and often thin pen) assumed four grades: hybrid (which introduced certain higher grade letter-forms, notably the half-uncial 'oc' form of **a**, into a formally written minuscule); set (a carefully written minuscule with frequent pen-lifts (*see* **39, 40**)); cursive (the basic grade, written with average care and speed and often featuring linking strokes and occasional loops (*see* **42**)); current (the most rapidly written).

Choice of script was primarily dictated by the nature of the work, with, generally, formal (majuscule) scripts for biblical and liturgical texts and minuscules for library and school-books and any other works. From the late 8th century, however, there was a tendency in Southumbria to favour mixed or hybrid forms which achieved prestigious, calligraphic effect for less effort. Documents were sometimes written in uncials at the beginning of the period, but during the 8th century minuscules became the rule, the heightened litigation of the early 9th century producing experiments with elaborate cursive minuscules (such as 'mannered minuscule' (*see* **8**)) which would impress in the courts and which were also deemed suitable for book use, challenging the traditional hierarchy (paralleling developments on the Continent where caroline minuscule was emerging as a standard multi-purpose script).

The pointed cursive minuscule favoured in Southumbria during the first half of the 9th century (*see* **42**) weathered the Viking storm and was adopted as the basic text script (with square capitals for display purposes) during the Alfredian revival. During the first quarter of the 10th century this 'pointed minuscule' (*see* **11, 41**) gave way to a 'square minuscule', assuming greater breadth, angularity, uniformity and a more upright appearance (seen, for example, in parts of the Parker Chronicle and the Tollemache Orosius (*see* **27**)). These modifications may have been stimulated by some early influence from Continental caroline minuscule, although some input from Insular half-uncial is also possible. Capitals and uncials also remained in use, primarily as display scripts.

Major Continental influence accompanied the reforms of Edgar's reign (957-75). Caroline minuscule (*see* **26**) had spread throughout much of Europe during the 9th century, only England and Spain resisting it, perhaps because they had scripts of their own which had already confronted the problems of legibility and uniformity which caroline minuscule had been devised to solve, and also because they were not under immediate Carolingian rule. However 'English caroline' was introduced, along with other Continental features of manuscript production,

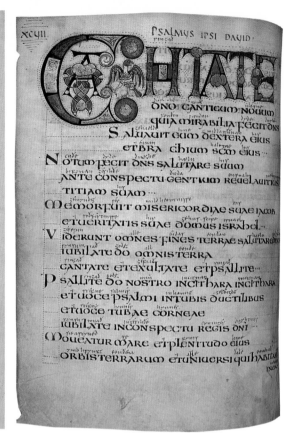

55 The Lindisfarne Gospels

c.700; Lindisfarne.

Initial **P**, with zoomorphic terminals, and display script. The text was written in 'Phase II' half-uncial by the artist-scribe, Eadfrith. The inter-linear Old English gloss (or translation) was added *c*.970 by a later member of Cuthbert's community, Aldred, who recorded the names of those thought to have been responsible for the original manufacture of the book in a colophon.

British Library, Cotton MS Nero D.IV, f.5v.

56 The Vespasian Psalter

8th cent., second quarter; Canterbury, St Augustine's.

Southumbrian style initial **C** and display script. Text is written in a romanizing uncial of Canterbury style. The minuscule inter-linear Old English gloss, of mid-9th-century date, represents the oldest extant translation into English of a biblical text.

British Library, Cotton MS Vespasian A.I, f.93v.

from the mid-10th century and continued throughout the 11th. Its use was, nonetheless, restricted to Latin texts, with Anglo-Saxon square minuscule continuing to be used for the vernacular. A number of bilingual books and documents contain both (*see* **31**), and square minuscule features often contaminate caroline (as in **38**). As during the Insular period, scribes would be expected to master the range of scripts, but several principal scriptoria producing English caroline have been identified: St Augustine's and Christ Church, Canterbury; Abingdon; Winchester (Old Minster); Worcester; Exeter. Two distinct styles of English caroline have been identified: Style I, in houses reformed by St Aethelwold (e.g. Abingdon and Winchester), a firm, broad, rounded script exhibiting little English influence and persisting from *c*.950 to the late 11th century (seen in the

Benedictional of St Aethelwold (*see* **36**)); Style II, a small, elegant caroline, perhaps modelled upon a distinct Continental school but influenced by Anglo-Saxon square minuscule, which is associated with St Dunstan at Glastonbury and Canterbury. This occurs throughout the second half of the 10th century and was perfected at Christ Church in the early 11th (*see* **73**). The opulence of book decoration during this period (coupled with the Anglo-Saxon love of calligraphy) led to an increasingly decorative and calligraphic treatment of English caroline, somewhat at odds with its basic character, throughout the 11th century (seen at its best in the work of Eadui Basan (as in **24**)).

Meanwhile, Anglo-Saxon minuscule continued to flourish. During the first half of the 11th century the square form gave way to 'round minuscule' (*see* **31**). Influenced by the rounded, deliberate character of caroline, it was nonetheless again characterized by a calligraphic, mannered treatment.

The Conquest did not terminate indigenous Anglo-Saxon scripts, and the Continental caroline written by Norman personnel may be readily identified in centres such as Durham. A distinguishing feature of Norman caroline is to terminate down strokes with a fine stroke rising sharply, whilst English caroline applies horizontal or near-horizontal serifs to feet. The latter is also generally more upright and lengthens ascenders and descenders.

Anglo-Saxon round minuscule, descended from its early Insular forebear, continued in use to *c.*1200, only relinquishing its distinctive features and letter-forms in favour of more general caroline characteristics from the mid-12th century to form an English expression of the new Protogothic (early Gothic, or Romanesque) script. In Ireland the scripts which it had played so great a role in evolving during the 7th century continued to be used, with various modifications, into the 20th century.

It should also be noted that Insular manuscripts made a distinctive contribution to punctuation (using several systems including the Mediterranean *per cola et commata* form (*see* **57**) in which line length clarifies sense, and an essentially Irish system of *distinctiones* (*see* **42**, **69**) in which a rising number of points denotes a rising value of pause) and to word division (developed primarily by the Irish to assist in learning the new Latin language). Abbreviations, including some short-hand symbols devised by Cicero's secretary, Tiro, were also extremely popular (with some characteristic Insular forms) and some distinctive orthographic variants occur (e.g. confusion of single and double 's').

57 The Ceolfrith Bible (Middleton Leaves)
Late 7th cent. (?), pre 716; Wearmouth / Jarrow.

Leaves from one of the two companion Bibles to the Codex Amiatinus (*see* **49**). They were used as wrappers for Lord Middleton's estate documents (to which the lower inscriptions refer). The script is a stately, romanizing uncial. Punctuation is *per cola et commata*, with line length serving to clarify the sense.
British Library, Add. MS 45025, f.2v.

Illustration and ornament

The Anglo-Saxon period may be divided into several phases in terms of cultural development, and especially where decoration and script are concerned. The phase from the late sub-Roman period (say *c*.550) and prior to the Alfredian revival and its aftermath (say *c*.900) is often termed 'Insular', in recognition. of the close cultural interaction of Britain and Ireland. The term 'Hiberno-Saxon' is also used to denote the area of closest overlap - Ireland, Scotland and Northumbria (with its influence also being felt abroad in the mission-fields). 'Northumbrian' and 'Southumbrian' (denoting the areas north and south of the Humber, rather than political units) also denote the two predominant cultural divisions of England at this time, although they obviously interacted. The period following *c*.900 is generally termed 'Anglo-Saxon' in artistic terms (denoting a pan-English, rather than a largely Anglo-Saxon/Celtic cultural environment).

A characteristic feature of Insular illumination is the integration of decoration, script and text. The earliest example of such decoration occurs in Codex Usserianus Primus in the late 6th-early 7th century and consists of colophon decoration (simple graphic marks and lines, often in red, designed to emphasise the major textual divisions), in this case a *Chi-rho* symbol (composed of **X** and **P**, the first two letters of 'Christ' in Greek) surrounded by decorative boxes. The next major early 7th century (Irish) monument, the Cathach of Culumcille, begins to incorporate the Celtic love of ornament into the new vehicle - the book. It features enlarged pen-drawn initials adorned with Celtic motifs (peltas, trumpet spirals etc., known as 'ultimate La Tène' as they are derived from the Celtic Iron Age culture of that name (*see* 1)) and with Christian symbols (crosses and fish) culled from near-contemporary Roman books. The script following the initials gradually descends in scale to the size of the text hand, a feature termed

'diminuendo'. The scene was thus set for the development of the Insular decorated initial, which was to exert a major influence upon later medieval manuscript art. These initials soon acquired more elaborate ornament, including beast-headed terminals (*see* 55), and the earliest examples of western historiated initials (which contain a scene illustrating the text) are found in the Vespasian Psalter (**59**) (a Canterbury product of *c*.730) and the Leningrad Bede (made at Wearmouth/Jarrow around the same time). Nor was the Insular contribution to the decorative articulation and elucidation of text limited to this. Line-fillers (decorative devices used to fill the end of lines which remain short, perhaps to emphasise a verse-form or the like) and run-over symbols (similar, but used to allow the remainder of short lines of text to be filled by text which is over-run from an adjacent line, the symbol serving to distinguish the two separate parts of the text occurring on the same line) appear to have been developed in Southumbria during the latter part of the 8th century. These consist of abstract symbols (sometimes resembling dumb-bells) or little beasts or figures. In the Book of Cerne (**42**) (a Mercian book of *c*.820-40) these form a menagerie of brontosaurus-like creatures (unkindly described as 'pretentious worms') which batten happily on the surrounding script. These devices also feature prominently in the Book of Kells (**61**) and, from the 9th century, became very popular in Ireland.

In addition to this minor decoration, major components were also introduced to emphasise the beginnings of texts. In the Book of Durrow (**1**), the first of the great Hiberno-Saxon Gospel-books, probably dating to the latter part of the 7th century, the distinctive Insular programme for introducing each Gospel emerges. A carpet page (a page of abstract design, although crosses may be woven into the design, named for their resemblance to eastern carpets (*see* 1)), probably of Coptic (Egyptian) inspiration, marks the text break, with a full-page symbol of the appropriate evangelist (Matthew the Man, Mark the Lion, Luke the Calf or Bull and John the Eagle, derived from the vision of Ezekiel). The depictions of the evangelists were to assume several forms in Insular art: zoomorphic (the beast symbols (*see* **63, 66**)); anthropomorphic (portraits of the evangelists in human guise, often accompanied by their identifying symbols (*see* **18**)); zoo-anthropomorphic (human figures with the heads of the beast symbols). In the Lindisfarne Gospels of *c*.700 the artist-scribe, Eadfrith, introduced the practice of depicting the evangelists as scribes (*see* **18**) – an extremely influential form, of Mediterranean inspiration. The opening words of the Gospels (*incipits*) (*see* **65**) were given enlarged major decorated initials, followed by decorative display script, and by the time of the Book of Kells (*c*.800 ?) (*see* **61,62**) the initials or first few letters or words had grown to virtually occupy the whole folio in a blaze of ornament (often incorporating details which were imbued with a symbolic meaning). Other less important textual breaks would also be marked by smaller initials and perhaps by panels of display script (display or continuation panels) (*see* **42, 55**). From the Book of Durrow onwards canon tables (a Gospel concordance system devised in the 4th century by Eusebius of Caesarea) were also subjected to a decorative treatment, often being set within arcades (*see* **53**).

The decorative motifs poured into the Insular melting-pot were largely drawn from the Celtic (ultimate La Tène) and Germanic repertoires (*see* **1, 65**) which had been evolved during the pagan past for use on metalwork, and occasionally stone in the case of the former. Celtic abstract curvilinear ornament was fused with Germanic interlace, inhabited by a plethora of beasts drawn from both traditions (although the amorphous Germanic repertoire was initially predominant in works such as Durrow (*see* **1**)). Frankish art also contributed some influence (perhaps seen, for example, in the independent beasts favoured in southern English illumination, such as the Vespasian Psalter (*see* **56, 59**), which are liberated from the interlace which enmeshed their northern counterparts). The more naturalistic animals of Pictish art also seem to have exerted an influence, for example in certain of the evangelist symbols of the Book of Durrow, and the Lindisfarne Gospels (*see* **55, 65**) heralded the arrival of a new brand of more identifiable birds, dogs and cats into Hiberno-Saxon art.

Antique, Mediterranean and Oriental art also exerted an influence. The vinescrolls (symbolic of the eucharist and often inhabited by the beasts of creation) so beloved of the Anglo-Saxon artist had their roots firmly in Antiquity, and many other foliate motifs sprang from these or more recent exotic sources (*see* **48**). The mythical creatures which sometimes occur were drawn from similar sources and may often have been imbued with symbolic meanings drawn from texts such as the *Marvels of the East* (*see* **31**) and the *Physiologus* (the manticore, a human-headed lion, for example, being the harbinger of death). Classical and Italo-Byzantine influence also found expression in the painterly, naturalistic figure-style encountered in many illuminations, especially those from romanizing centres, such as the Codex Amiatinus (*see* **49**) from Wearmouth/Jarrow, the Vespasian Psalter (*see* **56, 59**) and the Stockholm Codex Aureus (*see* **68**) from Canterbury and the Barberini Gospels (*see* **10**), possibly a Mercian book. Narrative miniatures may be found (*see* **58**), in addition to evangelist portraits, such as the Crucifixion from the Durham Gospels (**64**) (Lindisfarne, *c*.700), the Last Judgement and Ezra the scribe from the Codex Amiatinus (*see* **49**), and David and his musicians from the Vespasian Psalter (**59**). Others may well have been lost (as indicated by the inscriptions in the fragmentary Royal Bible (*see title-page*), and the cycles of illustrations, now preserved only in Continental copies of Insular manuscripts of the Apocalypse and Sedulius's *Carmen Paschale*). The Book of Kells (*see* **61, 62**), a work whose

58 The Durham Cassiodorus

8th cent., second quarter; Northumbria (Wearmouth/ Jarrow ?).

An early example of tinted drawing, depicting David, from the commentary on the Psalms composed by Cassiodorus, a 6th century Italian statesman and founder of monasteries. The iconography may have been adapted from an image of Christ trampling, or being adored by, the beasts.

Durham, Cathedral Library, MS B.II.30, f.172v.

59 The Vespasian Psalter

8th cent., second quarter; Canterbury, St Augustine's.

David, author of the Psalms, with his scribes and musicians. The historiated initial to Psalm 26 depicts David and Jonathan and is one of the earliest examples of this form of decoration in western art. This is the earliest representative of the 'Tiberius' group of Southumbrian manuscripts.

British Library, Cotton MS Vespasian A.I, ff. 30v–31.

60 The Lichfield or Chad Gospels

Mid-8th cent. (?); Northumbria, Ireland or Iona (?).

St Luke, with his symbol, the bull. Stylistically and technically this manuscript falls between the Lindisfarne Gospels and the Book of Kells, but its date and place of origin are uncertain. The early 9th century inscription (an early example of Welsh handwriting) records that it was swopped for his best horse by Gelhi, who gave it to the altar of St Teilo (probably Llandeilo-Fawr, Carmarthenshire). It reached Lichfield in the 10th century, but it is unlikely to have been made here, or in Wales, as sometimes suggested.

Lichfield, Cathedral Library, s.n., p.218.

date and place of origin are hotly disputed (Iona, *c*.800. being perhaps the most popular theory), contains a number of miniatures including the Temptation (**62**), the Arrest and the Virgin and Child. These images have recently been shown to carry a number of layers of meaning, multivalence being favoured within Insular art and learning. Kells is virtually an encyclopaedia of Insular art, incorporating all the varied influences already referred to, as well as the possibility of some contemporary Carolingian influence (again, vigorously disputed), hence its controversial place in Insular studies, for it is 'all things to all men'. The Celtic and Germanic love of design is again encountered in the stylization and linearization of much Insular figural art (for example in Kells), but the probability of influence from

61 The Book of Kells

c.800 (?); Iona, or perhaps Ireland, Scotland or Northumbria.

The Genealogy of Christ from one of the great Insular Gospel-books, and perhaps the most controversial (along with the Book of Durrow). It brings together all of the influences current within the Insular world and is something of an encyclopaedia of Insular art. It is, therefore, 'all things to all men' and opinions as to date and place of origin differ greatly (Iona, *c*.800 being widely favoured). Here a merman grasps the name *Iona* and this has been cited in support of an origin upon Iona, which was however called Hy at this period. Nonetheless, *Iona* is Hebrew for 'dove' which is 'columba' in Latin, and an association with a house founded by St Columba (including Iona and Kells, the book's later home) remains likely.

Dublin, Trinity College Library, MS 58, f.201.

62 The Book of Kells

c.800 (?); Iona, or perhaps Ireland, Scotland or Northumbria.

The Temptation of Christ. Multivalence is an important factor in Insular thought and art. This image depicts Christ on the roof of the Temple (which resembles a reliquary) but it can be interpreted simultaneously as depicting the Communion of Saints, with Christ as the head of the body of the Church, a theme developed in liturgy and exegesis.

Dublin, Trinity College Library, MS 58, f.202v.

63   The Echternach Gospels

*c.*700; Lindisfarne.

The lion, symbol of St Mark, from one of the three great Gospel-books (the Lindisfarne, Durham and Echternach Gospels) thought to have been produced at Lindisfarne *c.*700. The artist-scribe who worked on the latter two of these has been termed the 'Durham-Echternach Calligrapher'. The book may have been sent as a gift from Lindisfarne to St Willibrord's new foundation at Echternach (Luxembourg).

Paris, Bibliothèque Nationale, MS lat. 9389, f.75v.

64   The Durham Gospels

*c.*700; Lindisfarne.

The Crucifixion, with accompanying angels and the sponge and spear bearers (Stephaton and Longinus). An early example of Insular illustration and a devotional image particularly promoted by the Insular world. The work has been attributed to the 'Durham-Echternach Calligrapher', a suggested contemporary of Eadfrith's within the Lindisfarne scriptorium.

Durham, Cathedral Library, MS A.II.17, f.38³v.

another late Antique style of painting which itself tended to linearize figures (*see* **5**), rather than modelling them in a painterly, naturalistic fashion, should also be noted and may have contributed to the treatment found in the Lindisfarne Gospels (*see* **18**).

Perhaps the most notable Hiberno-Saxon manuscripts were the great Gospel-books. The Book of Durrow (*see* **1**) and the Book of Kells (*see* **61**, **62**) stand at either end of the Insular period, both closely linked by features of their texts and perhaps from the same centre, for which Iona is a prime candidate, although these are the most controversial pieces of the period

and are often, alas, the subjects of rather nationalistic arguments concerning origins (demonstrating how valuable the term 'Insular' can be). Three splendid Gospel-books were also produced at Lindisfarne, *c.*700: the Durham (**64**) and Echternach (**63**) Gospels, both the work of an artist-scribe termed the 'Durham-Echternach Calligrapher', thought to be an elder contemporary and possible master of Eadfrith, the maker of the third such book, the Lindisfarne Gospels (*see* **18**, **65**). Other major monuments include the Cambridge - London Gospels (*see* **66**, **67**), the Lichfield or Chad Gospels (**60**), the Leningrad Gospels (although this idiosyncratic

work may also have been produced south of the Humber), and a number of books (including a series of remarkable pocket-size Gospel-books (*see* **69**)) made in Ireland and, in a couple of cases, Scotland (the Book of Deer) and perhaps Wales (the Hereford Gospels). Brittany also responded to Hiberno–Saxon influence, as did a number of Continental monasteries, notably those founded by Insular missionaries (especially Bobbio, St Gall and Echternach (*see* **7**)).

Southumbria produced a number of important illuminated manuscripts during the 8th and early 9th centuries, including the Vespasian Psalter (**56, 59**), the Stockholm Codex Aureus (**68**), three Mercian prayerbooks (the Royal Prayerbook (**39**), the Book of Nunnaminster (**40, 41**) and the Book of Cerne (**42**)), the Tiberius Bede (**9**) and the Royal Bible (*title-page*), with the Barberini Gospels (**10**) being an important influence within the group and perhaps also a member of it (the Gospel-book having been made by a collaborative team including Northumbrians and a Mercian). These form the nucleus of what is known as the 'Tiberius' group (from the Tiberius Bede (**9**), which stood upon a book case surmounted by a bust of the emperor Tiberius in the library of the bibliophile, Sir Robert Cotton, who died in 1631). The members of this group were produced in Kent (notably Canterbury) and Mercia (perhaps including Lichfield and

Worcester). Like their Hiberno–Saxon counterparts, the decoration of these books is closely related to that of contemporary metalwork, in this case of the 'Trewhiddle' style.

The Tiberius group was particularly influential during the Alfredian revival. Late-9th–early-10th century initials feature the beast-headed terminals of the earlier works, although they are now often given bodies too and are interwoven with a lacy foliage, perhaps inspired by that of Carolingian manuscripts from Tours and Metz (*see* **11, 22**). These 'mixed' type of zoomorphic initials have been divided into two categories: Type I (*see* **27**), featuring creatures (and also human figures) with full bodies; Type II (*see* **11, 22**), using only their heads. Both varieties also use interlace, and acanthus-like foliage of Carolingian inspiration. Type II may be subdivided into two groups: a), using thin black wiry lines for its interlace (*see* **70**); b), featuring a thicker interlace drawn in outline (*see* **34**). Initials of different types may be encountered in the same book, but generally Type

65 *(pages 64–65)*   The Lindisfarne Gospels
*c.*700; Lindisfarne.

Carpet page and opening of St Mark's Gospel. The 10th century glossator, Aldred, recorded the names of those associated with its production: Eadfrith (Bishop of Lindisfarne, thought to be the artist-scribe), Aethilwald its binder and Billfrith the Anchorite who adorned it with metalwork. It successfully fuses Germanic, Celtic and Mediterranean influences to form the fully-fledged Insular book.

British Library, Cotton MS Nero D.IV, ff.94v–95.

66 a and b *(far left and left)*

The Cambridge-London Gospels

Early 8th cent.; Northumbria.

This charred lion symbol of St Mark (**b**) forms part of a survivor of the fire which devastated much of the Cotton Library (which contained many Anglo-Saxon manuscripts) in 1731. Another part of the book survives intact and includes this symbol of St John (**a**)(Cambridge, Corpus Christi College, MS 197B). It exhibits influence from the Lindisfarne, Durham and Echternach Gospels and was itself an important Gospel-book.

66a Cambridge Corpus Christi College, MS 197B, f.1.

66b British Library, Cotton MS Otho C.V, f.27.

67 Facsimile of the Cambridge-London Gospels

18th cent.; England.

Script and initials from British Library, Cotton MS Otho C.V, prior to the fire of 1731. From a volume of early hand-produced facsimiles of medieval manuscripts commissioned by the scholar Thomas Astle, for use in his *Origin and Progress of Writing* (1784).

British Library, Stowe MS 1061, f.36.

68 *(overleaf)* The Stockholm Codex Aureus

Mid-8th cent.; Kent (Canterbury ?).

Opening of St Matthew's Gospel from one of the most romanizing of Insular illuminated manuscripts, which may have used the Augustine Gospels (*see* **5**) as a model. The inscription on f.11 records its redemption, for gold, from a Viking army during the 9th century by Ealdorman Alfred and his wife, Werburh.

Stockholm, Kungl. Biblioteket, MS A.135, ff.9v-11.

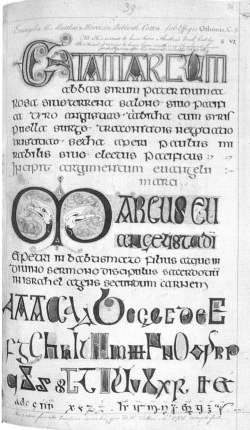

II focuses upon manuscripts of *c*.1000, whilst Type I runs throughout the period. These classifications were formalized by Francis Wormald, although recently attempts have been made to move away from an over-rigid classification. A different sort of initial was also introduced during the 10th century, composed of a rich, fleshy acanthus-like plant ornament derived from 9th-century Carolingian art. These are found at their finest in works of the so-called 'Winchester school'. During the 11th century these three essential styles fused to form the basis of the English Romanesque

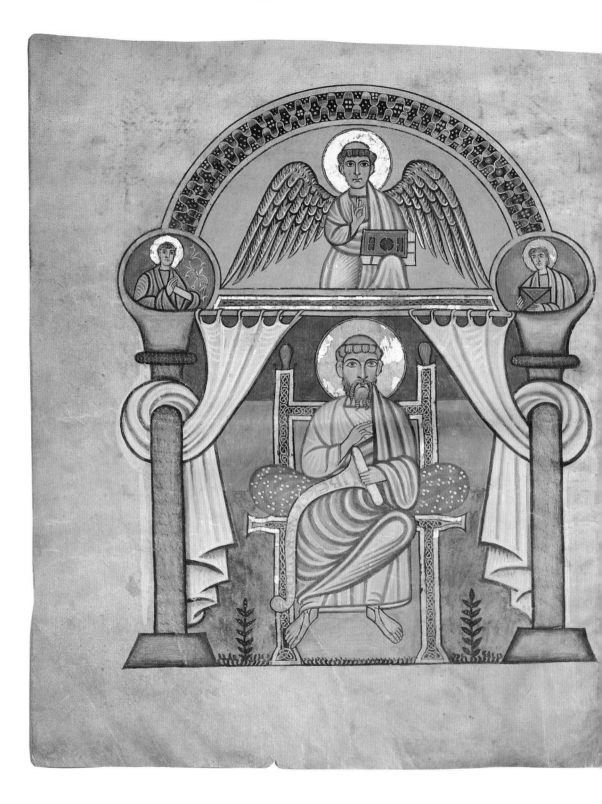

XP̄ AUTEM
GENERATI[O]
SICERATCUMESSETDS
PONSATAMATEREIUS
MARIAIOSEPANTECVA
CONVENIRENTINVENTA
ESTINVTERO HABENS

Ond yonðon ðepπ noldan ðæt ðaʒ hatʒanbeoc lönez, Indchie hæðhyyye punaðei, 7 nupillað heo ʒhætlan innπa chπty cipean ʒode toloye 7 topuldπe 7 toπ-bunʒa 7hiy ðπopunʒa todoncunʒa, 7ð̄ ʒodeundan ʒæh yeipe tobπucon de jncπnythchcipean ðæchplanhce ʒodʒ̄ yoy πchπað, cðbnʒhaðe ðt heomon apeðe chπpelce monaðe yon ælfπeð 7yon yhibuπyʒ 7yon alðhπyðe heoπa yaulum tobcum læt dome. ðahpile ðeʒoð ʒhπʒ̄on hæbbe ðt yulpihr bō ðoʒyπe yoyte beon moðe., ecyπpelce ic ælfπeð.dyx. 7yhibuπyʒ biddað 7halyiað onʒoðʒ̄ almæhtiʒey noman 7on allπa hiy halʒπa ðæt n.bnʒmon yeo todohʒeðπyπ ðæte ðaʒ hatʒan bloc ayelle oðde aðede ynomencπychch cipean ðahpile

69 Pocket Gospels

Additions of the 10th cent., second quarter, to a book of the 8th cent., second half; southern English (St Augustine's, Canterbury ?) additions to an Irish book.

The Insular cursive minuscule of the original book shows the degree of expertise achieved by the Irish in condensing text to a portable study format. The manuscript was 'modernized' for King Athelstan, its initials repainted (as seen here) and new evangelist portraits added (one of the originals being retained) in an English version of Carolingian Court School style.

British Library, Add. MS 40618, ff.22v–23.

initial, characterized by a lively, gymnastic quality (*see* **71**) which had its roots firmly planted in the Insular world.

During the second half of the 10th century two new styles of figural art emerged, both ultimately of a classical character but indebted to Carolingian interpretation. These were the 'first' or 'Winchester' style, distinguished by an opulent painting style with much gilding and colours, featuring much heavy acanthus–like ornament and a naturalistic figure-style in which the drapery often assumed a fluttering quality with decorative 'flying' hems (*see* **14, 72**). Ivories produced by Charlemagne's Court School are among the likely sources of this style. Insular influence was also reinforced by the re-importation of zoomorphic interlace in a formal and often rather static form popularized by Carolingian manuscripts of the 'Franco-Saxon' school, which had themselves responded to earlier Insular influence. The apogee of this style is seen in the Benedictional of St Aethelwold (*see* **36, 72**), made at Winchester *c*.971–84,

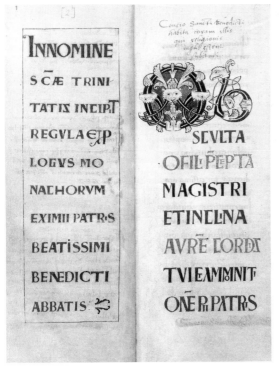

71 Isidore, *De Fide Catholica*

*c.*1000; Canterbury, St Augustine's (?).

This anthropomorphic initial S, composed of two gymnastic ecclesiastics, pre-figures later developments in Romanesque art. The script is an English caroline minuscule.

British Library, Royal MS 6.B.VIII, f.1v.

70   The Rule of St Benedict

10th cent., last quarter; Canterbury, St Augustine's.

Opening of the 'little rule for beginners' composed *c.*526 by St Benedict of Nursia as a blueprint for monastic life. It formed the basis of the 10th century English monastic reforms. Prior to this the heads of communities could determine their own regulations (often drawing upon the Benedictine Rule and / or those of other influential figures, such as Cassiodorus and Columbanus). The display script is composed largely of coloured square capitals and the initials are of Wormald's 'Type IIa'.

British Library, Harley MS 5431, ff.6v–7.

72 (*overleaf*)   The Benedictional of St Aethelwold

971-84; Winchester, Old Minster.

A magnificent book of episcopal blessings commissioned by Aethelwold, Bishop of Winchester (963-84) from the scribe Godeman. It epitomises the fully painted 'Winchester style'. This is the opening of the Easter blessing and depicts the Women at the Tomb. A connection between the image and liturgical drama has been suggested.

British Library, Add. MS 49598, ff.51v–52.

and this led to a primary association with Winchester, although the style is in fact found in other centres associated with the monastic reforms, such as Canterbury. In addition to the fully painted form, this style was also used for outline drawing, or tinted drawing (in which the outlines are coloured or the drawings are tinted with coloured washes) (*see* **36, 54**). Indeed, the first example of the style, the Classbook of St Dunstan of *c.*950, was executed in outline drawing, possibly at Glastonbury.

During the late 10th century the second major style was introduced to England, inspired by an important Carolingian manuscript known as the Utrecht Psalter. This had been made near Rheims, *c.*820, and featured a startling, agitated drawing style, indebted to a sketchy, illusionistic classical painting technique. The Utrecht Psalter was apparently available as a model, perhaps even in an unbound state, in the Christ Church (?) scriptorium during the early 11th

74

ab&erno &usque inater-
num supumentes eum
E tusticia illius infilios filioz
his qferuant testamtu eius
E tmemores sunt mandatoz
ipsius adfaciendum ea ;

Dns incelo parauit sede suam
& regnu ipsius omu dominabit ;
B enedicite dno Angeli eius
potentes uirtute facien
tes uerbu illius adaudien
da uoce sermonum eius ;

B enedicite dno oms uirtutes
eius ministri eius quifaci
tis uoluntatem eius
B enedicite dno oma opa eu
nonm loco dominationes
eu benedic Anima mea dno ;

CIII IPSO AUTO·

BENEDICANIMA
mea dno. dne ds meus
magnificatus es uehementer·
C onfessionem &decorem
induisti amictus lumine
sicut uestimento
E xtendens caelum sicut
pellem quitegis aquis
superiora eius ;
Q uiponens nubem ascensum

tuum quiambulas super
pennas uentozum ;
Q uifacis angelos tuos spc
&ministros tuos ignem
urentem ;
Q uifundasti terram super
stabilitatem sua nonincli
nabitur insclm saeculi ;
A byssus sicut uestimentu
Amictus eius sup montes

stabunt aquae ;
A bincrepatione tua fugi
ent auoce tonitrui tui
formidabunt
A scendunt montes &de
scendunt campi inlocu
quem fundasti eis
ermmum posuisti quenon
transgredientur neq con
uertentur operire terra ;

73 The Harley Psalter

Early 11th cent. (with later additions); Canterbury, Christ Church.

Psalm 103, from the earliest of three surviving English copies of the Utrecht Psalter, an influential Carolingian book (of Antique inspiration) made near Rheims, *c*.820, which was present in England and gave rise to the 'Utrecht style'. The differing responses of the various artists and scribes to their model is instructive: this artist followed it closely, enlivening certain details, whilst another hand has added new details (some drawn from contemporary local observation). This English copy also introduces more colour than the original.

British Library, Harley MS 603, f.51v.

century. There it inspired the first of three Canterbury copies, the Harley Psalter (73). A number of artists and scribes contributed to the latter, which was still being worked upon in the early 12th century. The challenge presented by a model distinguished by a complex layout and inter-relationship of image and text, as well as by a new artistic style, seems to have captured the imagination of the scriptorium members. Some artists adhered quite closely to the original iconography and technique, making only minor changes, whilst others frequently departed from it, incorporating features drawn from their contemporary surroundings (such as weapons, instruments, architectural details and the like – *innovatio* versus *traditio*, innovation rivalling iconographic tradition). A greater use of colour for the outline drawing was also introduced, in characteristic English fashion. Later work on the manuscript is in a lively, but less agitated style of drawing, known as the 'revived Utrecht style'. The influence of the Utrecht style may be seen in other early 11th century Canterbury works (notably in the Calendar illustrations of a hymnal, B.L., Cotton Julius A.VI (74)), but was not confined to this centre, Winchester works such as the New Minster *Liber Vitae* (15) and the Prayerbook of Aelfwine (23) also exhibiting its impact.

During the first half of the 11th century the two major later Anglo-Saxon styles, the 'first',

74 The Julius Calendar and Hymnal

Calendar early 11th cent., Hymnal mid-11th cent.; Canterbury, Christ Church (?).

A calendar in metrical verse preceding a servicebook. It is the earliest English 'occupational' calendar, depicting the labours of the months (in this case ploughing in January). Zodiac signs also occur. Calendars recorded the feast days of the ecclesiastical year (although obits and other events might be added). The drawings fuse the 'Utrecht' and 'Winchester' styles and the script is an English caroline minuscule.

British Library, Cotton MS Julius A.VI, f.3.

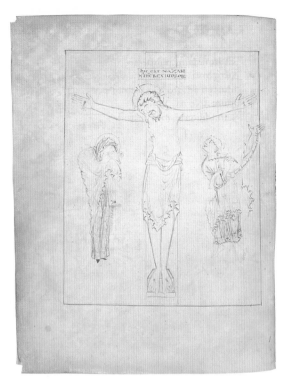

75 Psalter

10th cent., last quarter; Winchester.

This bold crucifixion miniature, with Virgin and St John, in tinted outline drawing, fuses the 'Winchester' and 'Utrecht' styles to produce a devotional image which is both monumentally calm and emotionally charged. The Psalter was a popular instrument of private devotion, as well as a servicebook.

British Library, Harley MS 2904, f.3v.

76   The Tiberius Psalter

c.1050; Winchester.

The Harrowing of Hell, from an influential prefatory cycle of Psalter illustrations of the lives of Christ and David. Its tinted drawings exhibit the manneristic tendencies of late Anglo-Saxon art. The 'Harrowing' was a popular English theme and an inspiration for early liturgical drama.

British Library, Cotton MS Tiberius C.VI, f.14.

or 'Winchester', and the 'Utrecht', began to fuse, with the monumental 'Winchester' style assuming a more restless, mannered character, executed in a more impressionistic painting technique, as seen in B.L., Harley 2904 (**75**), the Arundel Psalter, St Margaret's Gospels and the Gospels of Judith of Flanders. An accompanying heightened tendency towards pattern-making finds a dramatic expression in the Tiberius Psalter, a Winchester book of *c*.1050 which introduces an influential English cycle of prefatory miniatures (*see* **76**). One further element of 11th century stylistic development should be noted, namely Scandinavian influence. This is less marked in manuscript illumination than in other media, but Scandinavian zoomorphic interlace and foliate ornament, themselves largely inspired by Anglo-Saxon styles, do make a limited appearance in initials characterized by less disciplined, meandering interlace and somewhat stringy foliage which are indebted to the Viking

Ringerike style (seen, for example, in the Winchcombe Psalter).

Around the mid-11th century a harsh, metallic figure style (seen in the Caligula Troper (**77**)) makes an appearance in English art, perhaps as a result of German or Flemish influence, contributing to the transition from Anglo-Saxon into Romanesque art. The Anglo-Saxon contribution to medieval art did not however end here. From the late 10th century the Anglo-Saxon 'first' or 'Winchester' style was practised in the Franco-Flemish area, notably at St Bertin, whilst the Winchester style of border decoration found popularity in northern and western France, and was introduced to the Weingarten scriptorium through the patronage of Judith of Flanders. Normandy was particularly receptive to English influence (manifest in the Préaux and Jumièges Gospels) which was reimported following the Conquest.

In addition to the stylistic elements already discussed, Anglo-Saxon art contributed some distinctive iconographic forms to the artistic mainstream. The Crucifixion, the Trinity, the Evangelists and the iconography of Mary and of David all received particular attention and were developed as complex images, often invested with layers of meaning, some of which may be glimpsed through exegetical (or interpretative) commentary. These and other more idiosyncratic features, such as the horned Moses (derived from a misinterpretation of the biblical passage concerning Moses's descent from the mountain, having received the Commandments, during which he appeared 'radiant', mistranslated as 'horned'), were to continue to influence medieval iconography.

Thus, through a subtle web of cross-fertilizations, Anglo-Saxon and, indirectly, Insular manuscript painting made a major contribution to the evolution of Romanesque and, ultimately, Gothic art.

77   The Caligula Troper

*c.*1050; Hereford, Worcester or Canterbury (?).

A choir-book, containing the soloist's interpolations into the mass or the divine office. Contemporary inter-linear musical notation occurs. The script is an English caroline minuscule and the miniature depicting the naming of John the Baptist (note the wax tablet) is in a harsh, metallic style indebted to Continental illumination, heralding the Romanesque.

British Library, Cotton MS Caligula A.XIV, f.20v.

GLOSSARY

Ascender - letter-stroke which ascends above the top of most letters, e.g. the upright stroke of **d**.

Bifolia (*sing.* **Bifolium**) - double sheets of vellum which are folded to form the quire.

Canon Tables - a Gospel concordance system devised in the 4th century by Eusebius of Caesarea.

Caroline minuscule - a reformed script promoted by the Carolingians, which became the major bookhand throughout much of Europe from the late 8th century until the 13th in some areas.

Carpet page - ornamental manuscript page (sometimes incorporating a cross into its design), reminiscent of an eastern carpet. Generally divides the four Gospels.

Charter - document granting land or rights relating to it.

Chi-rho - an *XP* monogram denoting the first two characters of 'Christ' in the Greek, often used as a Christian symbol.

Colophon - inscription recording information relating to the circumstances of production of a manuscript (the place and / or people involved).

Decorated initial - initial composed of non-figural, non-zoomorphic elements.

Descender - letter-stroke which descends below the writing line, e.g. the tail of **g**.

Display script - decorative script, generally incorporating higher grade letter-forms, often used (along with an enlarged initial) to emphasise textual openings.

Evangelist symbols - the evangelists in their symbolic guise, derived from the vision of Ezekiel: Matthew the Man; Mark the Lion; Luke the Bull; John the Eagle.

Explicit - the end of a text.

Folio - a sheet of vellum, one half of a bifolium (can also be used to indicate volume size).

Hiberno-Saxon - term signifying cultural overlap between Ireland and England, of particular relevance to Northumbria.

Historiated initial - initial containing a scene or figure which illustrates the text.

Hybrid script - a compromise between varieties of script, mixing letter forms to achieve heightened status in return for less effort.

Incipit - the opening of a text.

Insular - term signifying the close cultural interaction of Great Britain and Ireland during the period *c*.550–900 and which sometimes obviates the need to differentiate between areas.

Interlace - plaitwork, much favoured in Germanic art and thereby introduced to Insular art.

Litterae notabiliores - enlarged letters within the text.

Majuscule - an 'upper case' script, whose letters are confined between two lines (bilinear).

Manumission - record of liberation from slavery.

Migration Period - *see* Sub-Roman Period.

Minuscule - a 'lower case' script, whose letters incorporate ascenders and descenders, occupying four lines (quattrolinear).

Parchment - term often used generically to denote animal skin prepared to receive writing, although it is more correctly applied to sheep or goat-skin, and vellum to calf-skin.

Pelta - a popular Celtic abstract motif resembling a triangle with one convex and two concave sides, named for its resemblance to an early form of shield.

'Phase I' - term applied to the Insular system of scripts to denote its earlier stages of development, prior to *c*.700 (although Phase I continues alongside Phase II in Ireland after this date).

'Phase II' - term applied to the Insular system of scripts in its fully developed form, from *c*.700.

Pricking - marks pierced with a point or knife into parchment to guide ruling for layout.

Quires - the 'gatherings' or 'booklets' of which a book is formed.

Scriptorium - writing office, generally (but not exclusively) of a church or monastery.

Serif - thin stroke sometimes used to terminate the main stokes of letters.

Slanted pen - pen with nib cut at right angles to the shaft, producing a less formal script with slanting heads and feet to letter strokes.

Southumbria - England south of the Humber, but not used to denote a kingdom in the way that Northumbria does.

Straight pen - pen with nib cut at an oblique angle to the shaft, producing a formal script with straight heads and feet to letter strokes.

Stylus - pointed implement, generally of metal or bone, used for writing on wax, may also be used for pricking and ruling layout on sheets of parchment.

Sub-Roman Period - 5th and 6th centuries.

'Tiberius' group - stylistic grouping of manuscripts made in southern England during the 8th and 9th centuries, named after one of its key members.

Trewhiddle style - style of decorative metalwork, featuring whimsical beasts and particularly popular in 9th century Southumbria. Named after typical pieces included in a hoard found at Trewhiddle, Cornwall.

Trumpet spiral - a popular Celtic abstract motif in which the end of a spiral is expanded to resemble the mouth of a trumpet.

Ultimate La Tène - Celtic curvilinear style of decoration derived ultimately from the Iron Age La Tène culture.

Vellum - *see* parchment.

Zoo-anthropomorphic - composed of human figures with beast-heads.

LIST OF MANUSCRIPTS CITED

Antwerp, Museum Plantin-Moretus

M.17.4 (Antwerp Sedulius, *Carmen Paschale*)

Cambridge, Corpus Christi College

MS 173 (Anglo-Saxon Chronicle or 'Parker Chronicle', Laws of Ine of Wessex and Alfred, etc.) pl.47

MS 183 (Bede's Lives of St Cuthbert) pl.12

MS 197B (Cambridge-London Gospels, with B.L., Cotton Otho C.V.) pl.66

MS 286 (Augustine Gospels) pl.5

MS 383 (Alfred and Guthrum's Treaty)

Cambridge, University Library

MS Ff.1.23 (Winchcombe Psalter)

MS Ii.6.32 (Book of Deer)

MS Ll.1.10 (Book of Cerne) pl.42

Dublin, National Museum of Ireland

S.A.1914:2 (Springmount Bog Tablets) pl.2

Dublin, Royal Irish Academy

s.n. (Cathach of Columcille)

Dublin, Trinity College Library

MS 55 (Codex Usserianus Primus)

MS 57 (Book of Durrow) pl.1

MS 58 (Book of Kells) pls 61, 62

Durham, Cathedral Library

MS A.II.17 (Durham Gospels) pl.64

MS B.II.30 (Durham Cassiodorus) pl.58

Exeter, Cathedral Library

MS 3501 (Exeter Book) pl.38

Florence, Biblioteca Medicea-Laurenziana

MS Amiatino 1 (Codex Amiatinus) pl.49

Hanover, Kestner Museum

WM XXIᵃ 36 (Eadui Gospels)

Hereford, Cathedral Library

MS P.I.2 (Hereford Gospels)

Leningrad, Public Library

Cod.F.v.I.8 (Leningrad Gospels)

Cod.Q.v.I.18 (Leningrad Bede)

Lichfield, Cathedral Library

s.n. (Lichfield or Chad Gospels) pl.60

London, British Library

Add. MSS:

11850 (Préaux Gospels)

17739 (Jumièges Gospels)

24199 (Prudentius, *Psychomachia*) pl.28

33241 (Encomium of Queen Emma) pl.16

34890 (Grimbald Gospels)

37517 (Bosworth Psalter) pl.35

40618 (Irish Pocket Gospels, modernized for Athelstan) pl.69

43703 (Burghal Hidage)

45025 (Ceolfrith Bible, Middleton leaves) pl.57

47967 (Tollemache or Helmingham Orosius) pls 27, 52

49598 (Benedictional of St Aethelwold) pls 36, 72

61735 (Ely farming memoranda) pl.46

Arundel MSS:

60 (Arundel Psalter)

155 (Eadui Psalter) pl.24

Campbell Charter:

XXI.5 (Writ of Edward the Confessor) pl.17

Cotton MSS:

Augustus II.61 (Synod of Clofesho) pl.8

Caligula A.XIV (Caligula or Hereford Troper) pl.77

Claudius B.IV (Old English Illustrated Hexateuch, or Aelfric Pentateuch) pl.54

Cleopatra A.III (Glossary) pl.6

Galba A.XVIII (Athelstan Psalter) pl.25

Julius A.VI (Julius Calendar and Hymnal) pl.74

Nero A.I (Wulfstan, *Sermon of the Wolf to the English*) pl.21

Nero D.IV (Lindisfarne Gospels) pls 18, 51, 55, 65

Otho C.V (Cambridge-London Gospels, with Cambridge, Corpus Christi College, MS 197B) pl.66 (see also pl.67)

Tiberius A.II (Coronation Gospels)

Tiberius A.III (Regularis Concordia) pl.13

Tiberius B.I (Anglo-Saxon Chronicle, or 'Abingdon Chronicle') pl.44

Tiberius B.V (pt I) (Calendar; Marvels; *Mappa Mundi* etc.) pls 31, 33

Tiberius C.II (Bede, *Historia Ecclesiastica*) pl.9

Tiberius C.VI (Tiberius Psalter) pls 32, 76

Titus D.XXVI-XXVII (Prayerbook of Aelfwine) pl.23

Vespasian A.I (Vespasian Psalter) pls 56, 59

Vespasian A.VIII (New Minster Charter) pl.14

Vitellius A.VI (Gildas) pl.3

Vitellius A.XV (pt II) (Beowulf) pl.37

Vitellius C.III (Herbal) pl.29

Harley MSS:

76 (Bury Gospels)

603 (Harley Psalter) pl.73

2506 (Cicero, *Aratea*) pl.26

2904 (Psalter) pl.75

2965 (Book of Nunnaminster) pls 40, 41

3271 (Tribal Hidage)

3859 (Nennius) pl.4

5431 (Rule of St Benedict) pl.70

Loan MSS:

74 (Stonyhurst or Cuthbert Gospel) pl.48

Royal MSS:

1.B.VII (Gospel book) pls 45, 53

1.E.VI (Royal Bible) title-page

2.A.XX (Royal Prayerbook) pl.39

6.B.VIII (Isidore, *De Fide Catholica*) pl.71

7.C.XII (Aelfric Homilies) pl.20

7.D.XXIV (Aldhelm, *De Virginitate*) pl.22

12.C.XXIII (Aldhelm's *Riddles* etc.) pl.34

12.D.XVII (Bald's Leechbook) pl.30

Stowe MSS:

944 (New Minster *Liber Vitae*, Alfred's Will) pl.15

1061 (Astle facsimile of medieval MSS) pl.67

Stowe Charter:

37 (Will of Atheling Athelstan) pl.43

London, British Museum, Dept. of Medieval and Later Antiquities

Blythburgh tablet and Whitby styli, pl.50

Monte Cassino, Archivio della Badia

MS BB.437 (Judith of Flanders Gospels)
MS BB.439 ("   "   "   ")

New York, Pierpont Morgan Library

M 708 (Judith of Flanders Gospels)
M 709 ("   "   "   ")

Oxford, Bodleian Library

Douce MS 140 (Primasius with Boniface marginalia) pl.19
Hatton MS 20 (Old English *Pastoral Care*) pl.11
Lat. lit. F.5 (St Margaret Gospels)

Paris, Bibliothèque Nationale

MS lat. 9389 (Echternach Gospels) pl.63

Stockholm, Kungl. Biblioteket

MS A.135 (Stockholm Codex Aureus) pl.68

Trier, Domschatz

Cod. 61 (Trier Gospels) pl.7

Vatican City, Biblioteca Apostolica Vaticana

MS Barb. lat. 570 (Barberini Gospels) pl.10
MS Pal. lat. 235 (Vatican Paulinus)

York, Chapter Library

MS Add.1 (York Gospels)

SUGGESTIONS FOR FURTHER READING

History and sources

J. Campbell, *The Anglo-Saxons* (1986)

P. Hunter Blair, *An Introduction to Anglo-Saxon England* (1977)

F.M. Stenton, *Anglo-Saxon England* (1989)

H. Mayr-Harting, *The Coming of Christianity to Anglo-Saxon England* (1977)

D. Whitelock, *English Historical Documents*, I (1979)

K. Crossley-Holland, *The Anglo-Saxon World, an Anthology* (1982)

Finding aids

H. Gneuss, 'A Preliminary List of Manuscripts Written or Owned in England up to 1100' *Anglo-Saxon England* 9 (1981) pp.1-60

N.R. Ker, *Catalogue of Manuscripts Containing Anglo-Saxon* (1957)

Art and Archaeology

C. de Hamel, *A History of Illuminated Manuscripts* (1986)

D.M. Wilson, *The Anglo-Saxons* (1981)

D.M. Wilson, *Anglo-Saxon Art* (1984)

C.R. Dodwell, *Anglo-Saxon Art, a New Perspective* (1982)

C. Nordenfalk, *Celtic and Anglo-Saxon Painting* (1977)

J.J.G. Alexander, *Insular Manuscripts, 6th to the 9th century* (1978)

E. Temple, *Anglo-Saxon Manuscripts, 900-1066* (1976)

G. Henderson, *From Durrow to Kells: the Insular Gospel books* (1987)

J.M. Backhouse, *The Lindisfarne Gospels* (1981)

J.M. Backhouse, D.H. Turner and L. Webster (eds), *The Golden Age of Anglo-Saxon Art, 966-1066* (exhibition catalogue, 1984)

J.M. Backhouse and L. Webster (eds), *The Making of England, Anglo-Saxon Art and Culture A.D. 600-900* (exhibition catalogue, 1991)

J.J.G. Alexander, T.J. Brown and J. Gibbs (eds), *Francis Wormald, Collected Writings* (2 vols, 1984-91)

D.V. Thompson, *Materials and Techniques of Medieval Painting* (1956)

R. Deshman, *Anglo-Saxon and Anglo-Scandinavian Art: an Annotated Bibliography* (1984)

Palaeography and Codicology

D. Jackson, *The Story of Writing* (1981)

M.P. Brown, *A Guide to Western Historical Scripts from Antiquity to 1600* (1990)

E.A. Lowe, *Codices Latini Antiquiores* (11 vols and suppl., 1934-72)

J.M. Bately, M.P. Brown and J. Roberts (eds), *A Palaeographer's View, Selected Writings of Julian Brown* (1991, forthcoming)

Gazeteers

L. and J. Laing, *A Guide to the Dark Ages Remains in Britain* (1979)

N. and M. Kerr, *A Guide to Anglo-Saxon Sites* (1982)

ACKNOWLEDGEMENTS

The author wishes to acknowledge the assistance of the following, in supplying photographs and other essential support: The British Library Board; The Trustees of the British Museum; Biblioteca Apostolica Vaticana, Vatican City; Biblioteca Medicea-Laurenziana, Florence; Bibliothèque Nationale, Paris; Bodleian Library, Oxford; Cambridge University Library; The Master and Fellows of Corpus Christi College, Cambridge; The Dean and Chapter, Durham Cathedral; The Dean and Chapter, Exeter Cathedral; The Dean and Chapter, Lichfield Cathedral; The Dean and Chapter, Trier Cathedral; Kungl. Biblioteket, Stockholm; National Museum of Ireland; Trinity College Library, Dublin; Harvey Miller Publishers; The Green Studio, Dublin; Rackhams of Lichfield; Dr M.O. Budny; colleagues in the British Library, Dept. of Manuscripts, notably Janet Backhouse, Mike Boggan, Frank Burton and the library assistants; Annie Gilbert and the British Library Photographic Section; David Way; Anne Young; Leslie Webster; Nancy Netzer; William Noel; Cecil Brown.